D1735886

Susanne Rank (ed.)

International Human Resource Management:

Concepts and Research

Shaker Verlag

Aachen 2016

Bibliografische Information der Deutschen Nationalbibliothek
Die Deutsche Nationalbibliothek verzeichnet diese Publikation in der Deutschen Nationalbibliografie; detaillierte bibliografische Daten sind im Internet über http://dnb.d-nb.de abrufbar.

ISBN 978-3-8440-4252-8

Shaker Verlag GmbH • Postfach 101818 • 52018 Aachen
Telefon: 02407 / 95 96 - 0 • Telefax: 02407 / 95 96 - 9
Internet: www.shaker.de • E-Mail: info@shaker.de

PREFACE

In our dynamic and globalized economy, the gap between international, standardized, and digitalized business processes and the local needs of customers is managed by people who collaborate together internationally. Thus, human resource management is a key success factor in an international company if functional networks around the globe are supposed to work together effectively.

The function of Human Resource Management (HRM) is to support managers and employees alike to be committed to their work, as well as to work effectively and efficiently. In general, HRM deals with all HRM topics that can come up in work life. In international companies, corporate HRM covers HRM concepts on an international basis. Whereas local HR managers transfer the global HRM concepts and processes into local demands and adjust them if required and possible. The crucial issue deals with the question of how much a specific HR process should be standardized or localized according to national demands of local labor law or culture. A good example is the recruiting process, especially if an expatriate is sought for a new subsidiary. Another HR concept could be Diversity Management: How people work together in diverse teams at an international scale or in a local subsidiary. This book provides international HR managers and HR researchers with IHRM concepts by combining research with best practice approaches of several international companies.

The first major section of this book (including the chapters 1-4) covers specific IHRM concepts and research from an international perspective. The second section of the book (including the chapters 6-7) focuses on HR processes aiming at an increase in productivity, or focusing on lean HR processes.

In chapter 1, *Prof. Dr. Susanne Rank* (University of Applied Sciences Mainz) introduces the different IHRM frameworks and the comparative HRM debate on convergence vs. divergence of HR best practices.

In the chapter 2, *Prof. Dr. Sabine Bacouël-Jentjens* (ISC Paris Business School, France) introduces her research on the impact of local national culture on European

Diversity. She compares the impact of French vs. Danish national culture on Diversity Management (DM) in French vs. Danish companies. It turns out that diversity in the company varies in different approaches, e.g. gender quotas, and is impacted by the local understanding of DM and legal requirements. The most effective DM appears to encourage a culture that values differences.

Prof. Dr. Sylwia Przytula (University of Wroclaw, Poland) focuses in chapter 3 on self-initiated expatriation as a new trend in international HRM. The main topics are how to classify self-initiated vs. posted expatriates and what the impact on HR expatriation policies will be.

Dr. Katarzyna Tracz-Krupa (University of Wroclaw, Poland) presents the results of her research about Employee Development within the European Social Fund in Poland in chapter 4. It evaluates the EU grant impact on small and medium sized companies concerning how to set up, implement and monitor the employee development program.

In chapter 5, *Prof. Dr. Susanne Rank* reviews the generational differences in work values, traits and leadership motivation. The generational impact on HR concepts as well as the interaction of different cultures and generations is discussed.

Which role does HRM play when it comes to increasing companies' productivity? Chapter 6 discusses this aspect by using results from a meta-study by *Prof. Dr. Ulrich Schüle* of the University of Applied Sciences Mainz. Increasing overall job-satisfaction should be a starting point for all HR departments. He presents current HR research studies on training and employee participation in regards to whether these concepts increase employee productivity.

Taking up the point of standardization, *Carolin Grode* discusses in chapter 7 global HR optimization through lean HR processes. She points out that the challenge in optimizing HR processes is to distinguish between administrative tasks, which can be standardized, and consulting and creative tasks, which should not be standardized. Based on her experiences as a global HR project lead piloting she summarizes eight success factors on lean management for selected HR processes.

All chapters of this book were subjected to a double blind review process. All authors appreciate the efforts of the following reviewers and thank them very much for their time:

Dr. Vincent Cassar, Associate Professor, University of Malta, Spain

Prof. Dr. Francoise Contreas, University of del Rosario, Bogota, Columbia

Prof. Dr. Chris Howard, Pfeiffer University in Charlotte, USA Prof. Dr. Michael Morley, Limerick University, UK

Dr. hab. Małgorzata Rozkwitalska, Associate Professor, Higher School of Banking in Gdansk, Poland

Dr. Joanna Purgał-Popiela, Krakow University of Economics, Poland

Prof. Dr. Armin Trost, University of Applied Sciences Furtwangen, Germany

This IHRM book is based on a collaborative IHRM project within the framework of the International Week 2016 of the University of Applied Sciences Mainz and the IHRM conference on April, 27th 2016 hosted by the School of Business. The IHRM conference was coordinated by the conference committee, consisting of Prof. Dr. Susanne Rank and Theresa Teichmann, HRM Section of our Business School.

The editor would like to thank all authors for their cooperation and contributing their articles. Furthermore, creating an IHRM research network across European countries was a great benefit and is an excellent starting point for further research collaborations.

Moreover, the editor would like to thank Theresa Teichmann for organizing the IHRM conference and Sandra Seibold for formatting this book.

Susanne Rank

Mainz, November 2016

TABLE OF CONTENTS

1 INTRODUCTION TO INTERNATIONAL HUMAN RESOURCE MANAGEMENT: CONVERGENCE OR DIVERGENCE OF HRM

Susanne Rank

TABLE OF CONTENTS

Abstract

This chapter provides an overview as to the definition of International Human Resource Management as well as regarding previous and current IHRM frameworks. Further, current studies are summarized to point out which IHRM processes could be standardized in European subsidiaries of an international company. Finally, the conclusion is drawn that a holistic IHRM pre-analysis is necessary before setting up universal, mandatory HRM processes in Europe.

Mail contact: susanne.rank@hs-mainz.de

1   Definition of Human Resource Management

The function *Human Resource Management* (HRM) deals with the administration of employee contracts and their individual data as well as the consultancy of the employees and managers along the employee life cycle (see Ulrich, 2005). Figure 1 gives an overview about the specific HR functions in form of a HR process map. The overall HRM goals are to support the managers and employees in a company or an organization to increase their productivity and their organizational commitment in terms of retention management. Additionally, the complementary goal is to ensure the excellent outcomes of these specific HRM processes in a cost efficient manner.

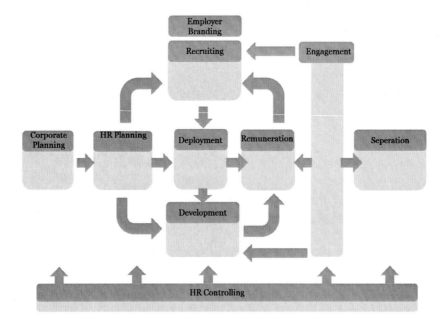

Figure 1: HRM process map along the employee life-cycle by Christ, 2015

Starting with the HRM planning, which is linked with the corporate planning of a company, the manager needs to figure out how he/she should recruit, deploy and develop or lay off his/her employees. These processes should be defined, implemented, supported and evaluated by the specific HRM functions of the

HRM department. In addition, the job grades of the compensation and benefit system should be defined in a fair manner in comparison to the job requirements and the competitors of the specific sector. Finally, a company policy should be implemented as to how the company deals with the natural or forced separation/ layoff process of the employees.

2   Framework of International Human Resource Management

Due to the globalization of business, digitalization and industry 4.0 (Baur & Wee, 2015)[1] many multiple international companies (MNC) work simultaneously on an international and on a local level. These impact factors require an international and local perspective on the HRM processes. Therefore, in MNCs the HRM strategy should define which HR processes should be standardized on an international level as well as how flexible these HR processes could be localized. *International HRM* (IHRM) is defined by Brewster, Sparrow, Vernon and Houldsworth (2011, p. 13) as followed: "IHRM examines the way in which MNC manage their human resources across the different national contexts." "[…] The organization that manages people in different institutional, legal, and cultural circumstances has to be aware not only of what is allowed and not allowed in the different nations and regions of the world, but also of what makes for cost-effective management practices. To take one often-quoted example: performance appraisal system which depends upon US-style openness between manager and subordinate; each explaining plainly how they feel the other has done well or badly in their job, may work in some European countries. However, it is unlikely to fit with the greater hierarchical assumptions and 'loss-of-face' fears of some of the Pacific countries."

---

[1] Baur & Wee (2015) define Industry 4.0 as the next phase in the digitalization of the manufacturing sector, driven by four disruptions: the astonishing rise in data volumes, computational power, and connectivity, especially new low-power wide-area networks; the emergence of analytics and business-intelligence capabilities; new forms of human-machine interaction such as touch interfaces and augmented-reality systems; and improvements in transferring digital instructions to the physical world, such as advanced robotics and 3-D printing.

IHRM deals with how MNCs manage the demands of ensuring that the organization has an international coherence in and cost-effective approach to the way it manages its people in all the countries it covers, (universalistic or convergence) while at the same time ensuring that it is responsive to the differences in assumptions and in what works from one location to another" (contingency or divergence; Brewster et al. 2011, p. 14).

Pudelko, Reiche & Carr (2015) summarize the historical origin and development of IHRM. They argue that in 1980 the traditional view of IHRM primarily focused on expatriation and leadership development. Taking the example expatriation, the managing director of a new subsidiary in India could be hired in India in the 21st century and not – as was traditionally done - be sent as an US expat from the US headquarters to India. Further, the IHRM research expanded from the US research perspective to an international level, including the context factor, e.g. the impact of diverse European countries on HRM.

Research input of the strategy researcher (Perlmutter, 1969; further Bartlett & Ghosal, 1989) shifted the IHRM perspective from the home vs. host country perspective to a multi-international vs. global vs. transnational level. Depending on the business sector, the products and the customers of an international company, Bartlett & Ghosal (1989) differentiate between two dimensions of business strategy of an international company: local responsiveness vs. global standardization. The IHRM strategy and its subsequent IHRM processes are influenced by this specific business strategy. If a multinational HRM strategy is given, no standardization of HRM processes are defined, but the HRM processes entirely focused on the local requirements (HRM divergence by Brewster et al. 2011, p. 14). Global HRM strategy impacts HRM processes towards global standardized processes with no local adaption (convergence). The transnational HRM strategy combines both aspects by standardization of HRM processes as well as customizing towards local needs. Lastly, a national HRM strategy focuses on the local requirements of a country without international focus.

Concerning the effectivity and the efficiency of HRM processes standardization is necessary to increase the quality of the HRM processes and reduce necessary time and costs (see HR business partner model by Ulrich, 2005). However, from the change management perspective (Rank & Scheinpflug, 2010) getting the acceptance of the local HR managers is the important success factor. Therefore, one could recommend implementing corporate HRM processes in their subsidiaries via a transnational HRM strategy; i.e. by customizing the corporate HRM processes to local needs to gain the acceptance of the local managers in the subsidiaries. Main HRM processes designed by the corporate center of an international vs. global vs. transnational company are introduced hereinafter.

Moreover, the impact factors on the HRM strategy and processes are more complex than described above. The integrated framework of IHRM according to Schuler, Budhwar & Florkowki (2002) shows that, on the one hand, IHRM issues, functions and practices (see central box in figure 2) are impacted by the MNE's strategy; on the other hand, the IHRM[2] is influenced by exogenous and endogenous factors. As a consequence of this input-output framework (Schuler, Budhwar & Florkowki, 2002) the IHRM success should result in MNE's effectiveness. In contrast to figure 1, there are some of the HRM functions moved on an international level within the MNC. Six HRM practices are the core IHRM processes: planning, staffing/recruiting, performance appraising, compensating, training and developing and labor relations.

---

[2] Hereinafter the term IHRM is used as a generic placeholder for multi-national vs. global vs. transnational HRM as the specific HRM strategy depends on the company strategical assumptions of Bartlett & Ghosal (1989).

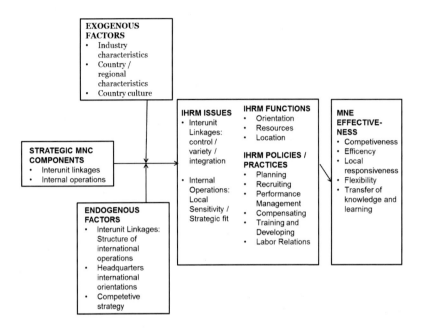

Figure 2: Integrative framework of IHRM by Budhwar & Florkowki (2002, based on Schuler, Dowling & DeCieri, 1993)

Bergman & Welch (2015) further developed the IHRM framework of Schuler et al. (2002) by including four organizational levels of the MNE defined as levels of analysis, i.e. macro, MNE, unit and individual level. Moreover, influential factors such as in the model of Schuler et al. (2002) are linked to the four analysis levels: culture, home vs. host country, individual experience. On the basis of the input vs. output model there are *proximal vs. distant outcomes* identified on each of the four levels. Organizational psychology research is combined with the financial perspective to create a holistic view on potential key performance indicators in a short- vs. long-term time perspective. The advantage of this overall IHRM framework of Bergmann & Welch (2015) is the link between soft and hard facts. For IHRM concepts and their definition of measures in MNCs, the matrix of four levels and two potential outcomes provides an excellent matrix and checklist for HRM implementation. However, Bergman et al. pointed out that further IHRM research is needed to support his proposed IHRM framework. Discussing further IHRM from an international to transnational level perspective, the cultural influences are mostly the barriers for implementation. Therefore, the next subchapter focuses on culture.

3   Convergence or Divergence of IHRM

As Brewster, Sparrow, Vernon and Houldsworth (2011) worked out that the IHRM departments of MNCs have to define how they structure their IHRM practices and processes regarding the universalistic vs. contingency approach by considering the impact of the global market and culture divergence. In contrast to the HRM in the USA, the European HRM research debate is about standardizing HRM processes in a universalistic approach (convergence) or localizing the HRM processes by considering the context/culture of the country (divergence). Moreover, both HRM approaches are possible in international companies. Scholz & Müller (2011) defined in their Di-Con-HRM model which parameters should be considered to know how much convergence of HRM is possible by focusing on Europe (see figure 3).

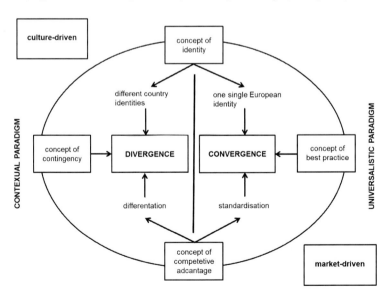

Figure 3: Framework of HRM in Europe – Di-Con-HR model by Scholz & Müller (2011)

The driving forces in this Di-Con-HRM model of Scholz & Müller (2011) are market and culture: On the one hand, HRM practices are driven by market and competitors' pressure, i.e. similar HR practices should be defined to overcome the external pressure resulting in a convergence across European countries (on the right-hand side of figure 3). On the other hand, culture influences HRM practices so that they should be localized (on the left-hand side of figure 3). Derived from the minimal group paradigm (social identify theory of Tajfel & Turner, 1979, 1986) and an important impact factor for HRM divergence is a strong identity with a preferred group, e.g. national culture. Tajfel & Turner (1979, 1986) investigated the social categorization of individuals: favoritism of the own in-group against the identified out-group. This minimal group research explains the power of group identity depending on which group is the focus for the group of comparison. Whether the affected employees in a subsidiary consider themselves as citizens of Europe (in-group) in contrast to the colleagues of the headquarters in the USA (out-group) or whether the in-group identity is German as opposed to e.g. the French group.

Mayrhofer, Brewster, Morley & Ledolter (2011) run a longitudinal analysis on human resource management in Europe in order to test the convergence vs. divergence approach. The study empirically analyzed the development of HRM in larger private sector firms in 13 European countries (Northern, Middle and Southern Europe) between 1992 and 2004. The countries were the impact factor (independent variables) for the convergence-divergence testing. Two sets of dependent variables were defined.

1. **HRM configuration** explores the approaches taken towards organizing and configuring HRM within the firm: Assignment of HR responsibilities and HR staff ratio

2. **HRM practices** are the activities pursued to fulfill the core tasks of HRM: Employee development, employee reward and employee communication

In summary, the results showed no convergence for all HRM variables. However, a *directional similarity* is supported across European countries for the following HRM variables: *assignment of HRM responsibilities* (moves towards the assigned HRM specialists), *employee rewards* (performance related and flexible pay elements) and *employee communication* (increased amounts of communication). Further, *no similarity* for *HRM-staff-ratio* and *employee development occurred.* Concerning employee development half of the countries increased and the other half decreased development because of cost saving strategies.

Transferring the results into HRM practices across European countries there is evidence that in these European countries HR specialists were assigned, comparable employee reward systems were implemented in local plants as well as similar employee communication strategies were applied to all subsidiaries. In contrast, employee development was localized.

Focusing on the IHRM model of Schuler et al. (2002) or Bergman and Welch (2015) the open issue is what drives the European HRM divergence found in the study of Mayrhofer et al. (2011): the different economic situation of the countries, the cultural differences or the different labor laws or mixture of all. A multiple level analysis is necessary. Moreover, Mayrhofer et al. (2011) identified the impact of a product regulated market on the European divergence of IHRM because this impact is correlated with employee protection regulation in a country. On the basis of that three country, clusters were identified which make a difference in local employee development resulting in no convergence.

4   Conclusion

A further research question is whether the trend for directional similarity of IHRM will increase for all HRM best practices/processes to achieve convergence in the European HRM approach. On the one hand, Mayrhofer et al. (2011) reported that the globalization index in Europe between 1992 and 2004 increased. On the other hand, one could argue that in 2016 the current national and political demands within the European Union (e.g. Brexit) drive the IHRM trend more in the direction of divergence of HRM in Europe, i.e. localizing the HRM practices.

From a global or transnational perspective, when opening up a new subsidiary or negotiating a joint venture in Europe as an MNC (e.g. Chinese company) an excellent HRM pre-analysis is required to understand the different European local HRM requirements if the divergence increases in the coming years. Further research on IHRM is necessary to empirically supported this by applying the holistic IHRM framework of Bergmann et al. (2015).

For the IHRM practitioner the change management success factor should be considered whenever a global or transnational HRM process like performance appraisal system or talent management is implemented: Define the corporate HRM requirements for local processes by 80% and give local degrees of freedom to the subsidiary to adapt 20% of the HRM process to their local demands. In this way the likelihood for the local not-invented-here syndrome is minimized and the divergence perspective of the discussed research is integrated. Furthermore, during the implementation phase the regional or local HR manager should figure on a multiplier or change agents for adaption of HRM process, later communication and training of the local managers. The informed and trained local managers as "end-user" of HRM processes trust their "own" local HRM manager more than the corporation's HRM managers. The local HRM managers understand the local culture and requirements and convince the locals effectively. Finally, the results of surveys carried on afterwards evaluate the local vs. trans-/international implementation success (see best practices of Rank, Grode & Krull, 2016).

References

Björkman, I. & Welch, D. (2015).Framing the field of international human resource management research. *The International Journal of Human Resource Management*. 26/2, 136-150.

Brewster, C., Sparrow, P., Vernon, G. & Houldsworth, E. (2011) International Human Resource Management. CIPD

Baur, Cornelius & Wee, Dominik (June, 2015). Manufacturing's next act. www.mckinsey.com/business-functions/operations/our-insights/manufacturings-next-act. 16/06/06.

Christ, Michael (2016). Lecture material of the Master Management, University of Applied Sciences Mainz, Germany.

Mayrhofer, W., Brewster, C., Morley M. J. & Ledolter, J. (2011). Hearing a different drummer? Convergence of human resource management in Europe — A longitudinal analysis. *Human Resource Management Review*. 21, 50–67.

Rank, S. & Scheinpflug, R. (2010). Change Management in der Praxis. Berlin: ESV.

Rank, S., Grode, C. & Krull, C. (2016). HR Excellence bei der SCHOTT AG - Globales Change Monitoring bei der Implementierung eines innovativen Performance und Talent Managements. In Rank, S. & Neumann, J. (Hrsg.). Change Monitoring. Wiesbaden: Springer Gabler Verlag.

Scholz, C. & Müller, S. (2010). Human resource management in Europe: Looking again at the issue of convergence. Paper presented at the 11th International Human Resource Management Conference, Birmingham, UK, 9–12 June 2010. http://www.orga.uni-sb.de/files/98.pdf. 03/15/16.

Schuler, R. S., Budhwar, P. S & Florkowski, G. W. (2002). International Human Resource Management: Review and Critique. *International Journal of Management Review*. 4/1. 41–70.

Schuler, Dowling & De Cieri (1993). An Integrative Framework of Strategic International Human Resource Management. *Journal of Management*. 19. 419-459.

Tajfel, H., & Turner, J. C. (1979). An integrative theory of intergroup conflict. In Austin, W. G. & Worchel, S. (Eds.). The social psychology of intergroup relations. Monterey, CA: Brooks/Cole. pp. 33–47.

Tajfel, H., & Turner, J. C. (1986). The social identity theory of intergroup behaviour. In Worchel, S. & Austin, W. G. (Eds.). Psychology of Intergroup Relations. Chicago, IL: Nelson-Hall. pp. 7–24.

Ulrich, D. (2005). HR Value Proposition. Boston: Harvard Business School Press.

PART I

IHRM CONCEPTS AND

BEST PRACTICES

2 CROSS CULTURAL RESPONSE TO DIVERSITY MANAGEMENT: DIVERSITY DISCOURSES IN FRANCE AND DENMARK

Sabine Bacouël-Jentjens & Liza Castro Christiansen

TABLE OF CONTENTS

Abstract

With increasing globalization, diversity management has emerged as an important workplace issue for many companies around the globe. Most of the extant research in diversity at the workplace has been conducted in the United States and may not represent the situation in other countries and regions in the world, such as Europe. The current research examines how the cultural, institutional, and specific business environments in two European countries – France and Denmark – which Hofstede's 5-D-model characterizes as culturally different and sometimes opposite, influence diversity discourses. Propositions on how these discourses impact diversity actions at the workplace will be formulated.

Mail contact: sabine.bacouel-jentjens@iscparis.com

1   Introduction

In contrast to previous generations, today's workforce in many countries has become more heterogeneous in terms of demographic diversity such as gender, ethnicity, nationality, religion, and age, resulting in the changing composition of modern organizations (Pugh, Dietz, Brief & Wiley, 2008). Diversity management as a concept originated in the US, starting with the Civil Rights Movements in the 1950s and gaining greater issues since the 1980s in response to demographic changes and international competition. Most of the extant research is, therefore, focused on the United States and its very specific diversity context. However, the issue of diversity management is rapidly gaining importance in Europe and has resulted on EU-level in the creation of numerous directives, mainly concerned with equality and non-discrimination issues. However, this common EU regulatory framework has not been interpreted and implemented consistently across EU-member states (Tatli, Vassilopoulou, Al Ariss & Özbilgin, 2012). Moreover, the adoption of diversity concepts throughout Europe does not occur at the same time as the enthusiasm for *diversity* or the concept of *diversity management* reflects major preoccupations of the concerned society at a certain moment of its history (Chanlat & Dameron, 2009). This is well illustrated by the contrasting picture on how Eastern European, North European and South European react towards proposed refugee quota in the context of the recent European refugee crisis (Robinson & Spiegel, 2015). Furthermore, diversity policies are not necessarily equally successful across borders (Bellard & Rüling, 2001). Authors studying international diversity management practices stress the importance of understanding the local responses to diversity issues, which emanate from national cultural and institutional settings including political, and legal contexts (Özbilgin, Syed, Ali, & Torunoglu, 2012; Syed & Özbilgin, 2009, Magoshi & Chang, 2009). Given the specific national histories and cultural dynamics of the European countries, they are likely to account for various diversity management models within Europe itself (Omanovic, 2009).

We aim at contributing to the debate on workforce diversity in Europe and on how companies could best manage this diversity for the sake of all stakeholders. For this purpose, our research focuses on diversity discourses in two European countries, Denmark and France, which are said to be culturally very different nations within the European region (Hofstede, 2003; Schramm-Nielsen, 2001). According to Tatli (2011), the analysis of diversity discourses is important because the discourse confers legitimacy for diversity practices. We will illustrate that French diversity discourses differ from the Danish ones by discussing the extent to which current diversity issues in Europe are addressed and resolved in these two countries. We contribute to diversity research by examining the field of diversity management from a cultural lens. In doing so, we try to broaden the still limited cross-cultural research on diversity in general and in Europe in particular, by proposing possible interrelations between societal factors and diversity discourses about gender, immigration and education in the two study countries which dominated discourses in both countries. Our work relies on extensive analysis of national statistics, existing legislation or legislative projects, institutions and associations and what they put forward to justify practice in terms of equality, non-discrimination and inclusion. From our observations we draw propositions on how national diversity discourses may influence companies' diversity management policies.

2   The national setting of diversity management

Analyzing diversity management within its societal embeddedness refers to diversity management in relation to other fields such as the cultural (social norms and values, culture), institutional   (legislation, education, industrial relations), and business environments (Tatli, 2010) and what is communicated in discourses for instance through political speech, legislation or legislative projects.

2.1   The cultural field and its influence on diversity management

The *cultural field* of diversity management refers to the historical and contemporary patterns explaining "inequality, subordination, representation and exploitation" (Tatli,

2010) and suggests, that diversity management practices vary across different historical, cultural and societal settings (Risberg & Søderberg, 2008). Denmark and France are different in terms of history and cultural values. Exploration of Danish and French culture through the lens of Hofstede's 5-D Model (Hofstede, 2003) shows – except for the dimension of individualism – significant differences and even puts both cultures on opposite ends for some dimensions. We can assume that these countries' perceptions of diversity and how they discuss and respond to diversity issues will vary according to their specific culture map.

Researchers characterize France as a bureaucratic and hierarchical society with high power distance (e.g. Hofstede, 2003; D'Iribarne, 2006), underlining the importance of status and affiliation to specific social groups. Children are raised to be (emotionally) dependent on their parents. This pattern of dependency will be transferred to teachers and later on to superiors building a society in which power is centralized and a fair degree of inequality is generally accepted. In contrast, Denmark is a society with low power distance where equality, egalitarianism, and fellowship are prevalent values (Hofstede, 2003; Holt Larsen & Neergaard, 2007). Power is decentralized and the country ranks high in terms of employee autonomy (Holt Larsen & Neergaard, 2007). Superiors and managers are less perceived as rule makers and controllers, but rather as facilitators who encourage collaboration and empowerment (Hofstede, 2003).

Ng and Burke (2004) suggest high power distance cultures to be associated with less tolerance and lower expectations of fair treatment and low power distance cultures to be more likely to value diversity.

The Danes score low on uncertainty avoidance, relying on much less structure and predictability and feeling less threatened by and being more tolerant toward different behaviors. In contrast, French score high on this dimension (Hofstede, 2003) and express a strong need for laws, rules, and regulations to structure life. Collectivist societies emphasize mutual obligations and protection regardless of individual contribution (equality norm). Both Denmark and France are individualistic societies which prefer distribution based on individual performance (equity norm) (Hofstede,

2003). The French combination of a simultaneously high score on power distance and on individualism is rather unique and leads to paradoxical situations in which subordinates formally pay respect to superiors, but may do the opposite of what they promised to do, as they may think that they know better, yet are not able to express so.

The Danish culture scores high in terms of Hofstede's (2003) fourth national cultural dimension, femininity, whereas in the French culture tends relatively stronger towards masculine values. In the context of diversity, feminine values focus on solidarity for the weak and inclusion, while masculine values support achievement, assertiveness, and material success (Hofstede, 2003).

Hofstede's fifth dimension, long-term orientation, describes how societies maintain links with their own past, while dealing with the present and future challenges. In societies with long-term orientation, such as France, pragmatic orientation prevails and people believe that truth depends very much on situation, context and time, and achievement of results calls for adaptability. Danes are a normative society, which scores low on this dimension, preferring to maintain traditions and norms, while viewing societal change with suspicion. In addition, short-term cultures focus on achieving quick results.

With regards to our case countries, we can assume that the predominantly opposite cultural orientations of the Danish and French societies open up into contrasting diversity discourses on various societal levels.

2.2 The institutional field and business environment: diversity discourses in France and Denmark

The institutional field, itself strongly influenced by the cultural field and, as a consequence, different in various national settings, produces institutionalized structures of diversity and equality in the form of legislation (e.g., anti-discrimination legislation), social dialogue between employers and employees, (non-) intervention of trade unions (Healy, Bradley & Mukherjee, 2004), and development of educational systems that ensure (un-)equal access to employability (Vermeulen, 2011). The *business field* describes organizations' business environment which may claim a more or less diverse workforce with regards to the specific customer behavior, production patterns, competitive environment and labor demand and supply (Tatli, 2010).

2.2.1 Masculine French and feminine Danes? Gender equality in the labor market

Theoretically, gender equality in Europe goes back to 1957 when the principle of equal pay for equal work became part of the Treaty of Rome. In 1976, the European Equal Treatment Directive required states to take measures to improve the equal access of men and women to employment, vocational training and promotion, and working conditions. However, inequalities in terms of employment rate, career advancement, and pay still exist but to different degrees in the various European countries. While the employment rate for men in Europe was 70.1 percent in 2014, for women, it was only 59.69 percent in the same year (Eurostat, 2015). In all EU-Member States, female employment rates are lower than those for males with big variations across the EU.

However, in France, women's labor market activity rates are slightly above EU average with 60.9 percent (Eurostat, 2015). Women are still underrepresented in management functions (European Commission, 2013) and, as Lewis & Humbert (2010) demonstrated, in technical and scientific occupations. A gender pay gap is still existent, although slightly below EU-level (Eurostat, 2013b).

Although gender equality appeared at France's constitutional level in 1946, husbands still had the power to prevent their wives from working until 1970. But with a growing participation of women in the labor market French gender policy evolved into a "working mother model" relying on considerable state support for working parents for the provision of childcare, highly developed parental leave policies, as well as tax incentives and family allowances (Fagnani & Math, 2009). These measures contribute to the fact that France has the highest fertility rate among EU-countries (Eurostat, 2012). A number of laws (Roudy Act in 1983, Genisson Act in 2001, law on equal pay in 2006) reaffirm the principle of equality throughout the professional environment, including recruitment, compensation, promotion, or training. In addition, the laws established the obligation of companies to produce an annual report on gender situation and encourage positive action in favor of women (Klarsfeld, Boysen, Ng, Roper & Tatli, 2014). Furthermore, an obligation was introduced to negotiate with social partners (unions, employee representatives) on equal opportunities at company and industry levels (Bender, Scotto & Hult, 2012). Implementing an EU directive in 2011, France set a 40 percent quota (to be reached until 2017) for women on boards of directors and supervisory boards. However, the legal framework offers French employers some room for interpretation and ways for partially complying with the law (Klarsfeld, Ng & Tatli, 2012) resulting in a contrasted picture with a high rate of full-time female employees relying on considerable state support for working parents, but with lower payments for female jobs and a still persisting glass ceiling in both the private and the public sectors.

In Denmark, a discourse of gender equality is prevalent and predominantly perceived as something already achieved. Universal welfare services and extensive childcare facilities have cleared the way for high female labor market participation (Rose, 2007). Women's employment rate equals 69.8 percent in 2014 and is significantly higher than in France (Eurostat, 2015). Laws on equal pay have existed since 1976 but policies of gender equality have been relatively weak and primarily related to formal anti-discrimination in the labor market. A strong focus is being placed on voluntary measures across the different dimensions of gender equality policies, legitimized by a discourse on flexibility and freedom of choice (Rolandsen Agustin, 2011). Active positive discrimination is not common practice and government policies do not invite to do so either (Emerek & Bak Jørgensen, 2011). However, even though Denmark is known to have a higher degree of equal treatment between the sexes, only little attention has been paid to female representation on Danish boards. In 2012, legislation was introduced for equal representation of men and women in boards and management in the biggest Danish companies, however, without setting any quotas (Blöndal & Bendixen, 2012).

We can observe that gender equality in France is more regulated than in Denmark, which might be partly explained by the opposite scores of both countries in terms of uncertainty avoidance.

2.2.2 Discourses on immigration and ethnic minorities

In Europe, France holds one of the longest histories of immigration, initially from European countries, later from former colonies in North Africa and more recently from Sub-Saharan Africa. Today, around 25 percent of the population has an immigrant background (large second generation and average-sized foreign-born population). Sixty-six percent of the foreign-born come from outside EU and 90 percent of these from low- or-medium-developed countries (Mipex, 2015). Despite of officially recognizing minority groups, France has always defended a universal model of citizenship, which does not acknowledge differences between citizens. This model of *universal citizenship* opposes multiculturalism (Tatli, Vassilopoulou, Al Ariss & Özbilgin, 2012) and leads cultural diversity to be a controversial concept. So far, the immigration concept has functioned as an assimilation process but this did not prevent widespread employment discrimination or the progressive constitution of ethnic segregated areas in poorer suburbs. The debate between integration and assimilation is still unsettled and takes a new dimension with the European context and its advocacy for cultural diversity. Indeed, in the name of equality of the citizens in front of the law, no difference of the individuals is taken into account if it is not the one of competence and, therefore, forbids any distinction of people according to ethnic criteria. The collection of statistics on ethnic origin is prohibited and renders the quantification of the proportion of immigrant people and the implementation of support measures difficult (Bender et al. 2012). However, the suburb riots of 2005 show that equal rights do not simultaneously provide equal opportunities nor equal treatment, and that certain populations remain to be put aside. Many studies have shown that ethnic minorities suffer from discrimination on the labor market (e.g. Bender et al., 2012). Although many non-governmental organizations such as the *Club du 21 siècle*, initiated in 2004 by entrepreneurs and senior officials primarily of foreign origin, and the *Charter of Diversity*, introduced in 2004 on the initiative of the French employers' organization, mark the voluntary commitment of parts of French opinion makers concerning non-discrimination and the promotion of diversity. However, France exhibits increasing votes for the far-right populist National Front Party and a sizeable minority of the public holding anti-immigrant attitudes (Mipex, 2015), especially in the aftermath of the 2015 Isis terror attacks in Paris (Rachman, 2015).

Compared to France, Denmark does not have a long immigration history. Until the late 1970s, the Danes considered workers from abroad as *guests* and *visitors* rather than as future citizens. In 2013, Denmark's total population of immigrants and their descendants was 11.1 percent. Most immigrants have a European or Asian background. (Danish Immigration Service, 2014). In 1998, an organization called *Foreningen Nydansker* (The Association of New Danes) was established on the initiative of human resource managers from several large companies (Wrench, 2002). With conferences and workshops they tried to establish links between the *new Danes* and the labor market, unions, employers' associations, and public authorities to facilitate their integration. However, immigrants with Arabic, African and Asian origins have had great difficulties accessing the Danish labor market.

2.2.3 Discourse on equal opportunities: Access to education.

Despite some loosening up in recent years, the French educational system is elitist and access to the precious private *grandes écoles* is still protected by severe selection processes where an analytical mind, intellectual rigor, and ability to synthesize information are valued (OECD, 2015). The attendance at a particular school may determine the future career path as educational and intellectual credentials serve as finely-tuned hierarchical discriminators (OECD, 2015). Access to power positions in public and private institutions is reserved for the so called French elites, and promoted by a highly elitist educational system. Accordingly, the principle of equal rights in France does not simultaneously provide equal opportunities. The *equality of rights*, emanating from the democratic principle, consists of granting the same rights to all without taking into account disparities of departure. For an example, non-EU-born are mostly low- or medium- educated (40 percent and 31 percent, respectively), although there has been a 5 percent increase in the share of university-educated in recent years (Mipex, 2015). The recent Pisa-study on education examines the impact of socio-economic background on school performance and criticizes a deterioration of equal access to education in France during the last 10 years (OECD, 2015) despite the French Education Authorities' implementation and promotion of actions to integrate more students from lower social backgrounds into the so called *grandes écoles* since 2001 (OECD, 2015). The youth unemployment rate, in particular of those with low or missing educational diplomas, is one of the highest in the EU (Eurostat, 2013a). In addition, the employment rate of older workers (aged 55-64), is well below EU-average with 47 percent in 2014 (Eurostat, 2015).

The Danish educational system is strongly characterized by the previously mentioned comprehensive welfare system, reducing the impact of economic resources on educational equality (Borchorst, 2008). Furthermore, the educational system combines an equality-oriented model with no tracking at the elementary level and no tuition fees in higher education with a strong vocational education path. Admission tests for upper secondary education were abolished in 2001. Elementary teachers only have recommendatory function when assessing students' abilities for this education path (Jager, 2009). The youth unemployment rate is one of the lowest in the EU (Eurostat, 2013a). The Danish government has made demands on private companies and public institutions to incorporate other ethnic groups into the Danish workforce and, at the same time, encourages employees to remain in the labor market longer in order to decrease the costs for unemployment, cash relief, pensions, and other types of transfer payments.

2.2.4 *Institutional actions as response to national diversity issues*

The French government tried to tackle the above-mentioned issues by implementing legal frameworks to guarantee equal rights and opportunities. In 2004, France adopted the European Council Directive (from November 2000), establishing a general framework for equal treatment in employment and occupation via a national law (Law no. 2004-1486) proclaiming successively the creation of new authorities against discrimination and in favor of equality such as the *Defender of Rights (Défenseur des droits)* and the *National Agency for the Social Cohesion and Equal Chances (Agence nationale pour la cohesion sociale et l'égalité des chances)*. In 2008, a diversity label is created at the request of the French State, to reward companies with strong commitment (Klarsfeld et al., 2012). Nationwide inter-professional agreements are also introduced to strengthen the fight against the discrimination in companies (for example, in 2004 for the equality of men and women, in 2006 on diversity, and in 2010 on seniors). Thus, policies enforced by legislation also incited companies to think about diversity. However, the French laws do not specifically adopt the term *diversity*; they rather refer to equality and anti-discrimination (Klarsfeld et al., 2012).

The Danish legislation has complied with the EU directives on equal opportunities and equal treatment of men and women when it comes to access to the labor market, vocational training, promotion, and working conditions. However, political discourses still focus on voluntary measures, legitimized by a discourse on flexibility and freedom of choice (Hvenegård-Lassen, 2009; Rolandsen Agustin, 2011). Lauring (2013) contends that business arguments for diversity management are often presented as being of voluntary character rather than as a set of moral and legal obligations. The business case argument for diversity management may divert attention from structural inequality and moral constraints in a way that legally yields a financial surplus. Promoting diversity as a business case as well as a social responsibility may prevail as a trend among larger Danish companies.

To summarize the national setting of diversity in our two case countries, we can say that in general, diversity discussions in the low-uncertainty-context of Denmark follow an approach of voluntarism, whereas discussions in the French high-uncertainty-context follow a mandate approach, addressing major diversity issues by the legal body except for the ethnicity issue. Due to differing immigrant history, the ethnicity issue is more dominant in France than in Denmark, but surprisingly less addressed (missing legal body, missing statistics), maybe reflecting a more pragmatic and adaptive orientation (long-term orientation) of the French. Although legislation regarding female employment in Denmark is less extensive than it is in France, the percentage of employed women is higher than in France which might be explained by the higher feminity score of the Danes. Furthermore, unemployment rates are lower in Denmark, reflecting more egalitarian access to education and work (in line with feminine and low power distance values, prevailing for the Danes).

We have discussed that the macro context of a society, i.e. culture, the socio-political factors, legal framework, demography and history (e.g., of immigration), inevitably determines discourses on diversity becoming salient in both society and the workplace (Syed & Özbiglin, 2009). In other words, the issues of diversity and discrimination that proliferate in the workplace should have their genesis in societal determinants of a nation. It will be interesting to see how the national diversity management discourses influence companies in Denmark and in France and how these companies respond to diversity issues.

3   Discussion and Propositions

Our findings suggest that different societal contexts in France and in Denmark shape companies' diversity practices in these countries. The comparison about French and Danish diversity discourses in the light of their respective cultural and institutional framework allows for the elaboration of some propositions how these discourses might influence companies in their engagements in diversity at the workplace. Here we develop three suggestions for more extensive testing.

Following this discussion about diversity practices being shaped by societal factors of the national setting, our first set of propositions refers to the influence of cultural values:

P1a: Companies in countries with high power distance favor top-down approaches when implementing diversity practices, whereas companies in countries with low power distance follow a bottom-up movement.

P1b: Companies in countries with high uncertainty avoidance adhere to more laws on diversity than companies in countries with low uncertainty avoidance. The latter may be more inclined to follow a voluntarist approach.

P1c: Companies in countries that score high on femininity focus more on inclusion.

We draw our second proposition from different immigration histories observed in France and Denmark and consequent discourses in this field:

P2: Companies in countries that experience high immigration from other ethnic and religious origins have a stronger need to integrate ethnic minorities in their diversity management program

Finally, we draw our third proposition from the national gender context as described above and the opposite scores of France and Denmark on Hofstede's Masculinity/Femininity dimension as follows:

P3: Companies that operate in feminine countries may be less concerned with gender issues in their diversity policies than those that operate in more masculine societies.

Our propositions of how societal level factors influence a company's diversity programs can fill the gap in our understanding of diversity management in Europe and further explain how societal and institutional factors shape European trends in diversity management.

4   Conclusion

Many researchers have recommended the need to extend the scope of the study of diversity management to different national contexts in order to assess the uniqueness of the findings. Our review of the literature revealed a few studies comparing two or more countries in Europe (e.g., Bellard & Rüling, 2001; Klarsfeld et al., 2014; Klarsfeld et al., 2012; Tatli et al., 2012; Wrench, 2002), but comparative field research at the company level within the European context still remains limited. Our work is limited to two European countries. Nevertheless, our comparison of French and

Danish diversity discourses through the cultural lens offers a perspective on how diversity initiatives are conceptualized, implemented, and communicated on national company level. Another limitation of our work lies in the limited focus on gender, ethnicity and education. Other diversity factors as for example age or disability also merit exploration. Future research calls for testing of our proposition through empirical work.

Practical implications of our research are manifold. We show that Europe differs significantly from the US-American context, so practitioners should be careful with the transfer of US-patterned DM-concepts. Within Europe, countries also differ culturally, so a European pattern of DM (based on EU-directives) should be adapted to national contexts. We were able to illustrate the importance of understanding diversity discourses in a national context. We hope that our research will enable diversity management practitioners to analyze diversity issues in a more complex way when implementing or transferring practices to a national setting.

References

Bellard, E., & Rüling, C. C. 2001. *Importing diversity management: Corporate discourses in France and Germany.* Geneva: HEC.

Bender, A. F., Scotto, M. J., & Hult, M. 2012. *Le Management de la diversité en France et en Suède: une approche compérative.* Paper presented at the conference "Le Management de la diversité", Lyon, France.

Blöndal, E., & Bendixen, J. K. 2012. Women on boards and women in management - A comparative overview of regulations in Iceland and Denmark. Reykjavik: University of Iceland.

Borchorst, A. 2008. Woman-friendly policy paradoxes? Childcare policies and gender equality visions in Scandinavia. In K. Melby (Ed.), *Gender equality and welfare politics in Scandinavia: The limits of political ambition?* Bristol: Policy Press.

Chanlat, J. F., & Dameron, S. 2009. *Management et diversité: Lignes de tension et perspectives.* Paper presented at the Annual Meeting Rencontres Internationales de la Diversité, Corté.

Danish Immigration Service. 2014. Statistical Overview Migration and Asylum 2013. Danish Immigration Service. Copenhagen.

D'Iribarne, P. 2006. *L'étrangeté française.* Paris: Editions du Seuil.Eurostat. 2009.

Emerek, R., & Bak Jørgensen, M. 2011. *Lige rettigheder - Ligestilling i Danmark.* Oslo: Det norske Likestillingsutvalg.

European Commission (2013). Women and men in leadership positions in the European Union, in 2013. Brussels

Eurostat. 2012 available at: http://epp.eurostat.ec.europa.eu/statistics_explained/index.php/Fertility_statistics (accessed 8 January 2016).

Eurostat. 2012b. available at: http://epp.eurostat.ec.europa.eu/statistics_explained/index.php/Employment_statistics (accessed 22 January 2016).

Eurostat; 2013a. available at: http://epp.eurostat.ec.europa.eu/statistics_explained/index.php/Unemployment_statistics (accessed 22 January 2016).

Eurostat. 2013b. available at: http://epp.eurostat.ec.europa.eu/statistics_explained/index.php/Gender_pay_gap_statistics. (accessed 2 January 2016).

Eurostat, 2015. Employment statistics. available at: http://ec.europa.eu/eurostat/statistics-explained/index.php/Employment_statistics (accessed 22 March 2016).

Fagnani, J., & Math, A. 2009. Policy packages for families with children in 11 European countries: multiple approaches. In C. Saracena & A. Leira (Eds). Childhood: Changing contexts. *Comparative Social Research*. 25: 55-78

Hvenegård-Lassen, K. 2009. Managing Diversity, *Migration, State and Pedagogy*. Roskilde Universitetscenter.

Healy, G., Bradley, H., & Mukherjee, N. 2004. Individualism and collectivism revisited: A study of black and minority ehnic women. *Industrial Relations Journal*, 35

(5): 451-466.

Hofstede, G. 2003. *Culture's consequences: Comparing values, behaviour, institutions and organisations across nations* (2nd ed.). Thousand Oaks: Sage Publications

Holt Larsen, H., & Neergaard, U. 2007. *Nordic lights: A research project on nordic leadership and leadership in the nordic countries*. Copenhagen: Copenhagen: Nordiske Kommunale Abejdsgiverorganisationer.

Jager, M. M. 2009. Equal Access but Unequal outcomes: Cultural Capital and Educational Choice in a Meritocratic Society. *Social Forces*. 87(4): 1943-1971.

Klarsfeld, A., Booysen, L. A. L., Ng, E., Roper, I., & Tatli, A. 2014. Introduction: Equality and Diversity in 14 Countries - Analysis and Summary. In A. Klarsfeld (Ed.), *Country Perspectives on Diversity and Equal Treatment: 1-12*: Edward Elgar Publishing.

Klarsfeld, A., Ng, E., & Tatli, A. 2012. Social regulation and diversity management: A comparative study of France, Canada and the UK. *European Journal of Industrial Relations*, 18(4): 309-327.

Lauring, J. 2013. International diversity management: Global ideals and local responses. *British Journal of Management*, 24: 211-224.

Lewis, S., & Humbert, A.L. 2010. Discourse or reality? "Work-life balance", flexible working policies. Equality, Diversity and Inclusion: An International Journal. 29(3): 239-254.

Magoshi, E., & Chang, E. 2009. Diversity management and the effects on employees' organizational commitment: Evidence from Japan and Korea. Journal of World Business, 44: 31-40.

Mipex. 2015. Migrant Integration Policy Index 2015. Available at: http://www.mipex.eu/# (accessed 19 September 2015).

29

Ng, E. S. W., & Burke, R. J. 2004. Cultural values as predictors of attitudes towards equality and diversity: a Canadian experience. *Women in Management Review*, 19(6): 317-324.

OECD. 2015. Vers un système d'éducation plus inclusif en France? Série «Poliques meilleures» France 2015. OECD.

Omanovic V., (2009), "Diversity and its management as a dialectical process: Encountering Sweden and the U.S.", *Scandinavian Journal of Management*, 25, 352-362

Özbilgin, M. F.; Syed, J.; Ali, F.; Torunoglu, D. 2012. International Transfer of Policies and Practices of Gender Equality in Employment to and among Muslim Majority Countries *Gender, Work & Organization*. 19 (4):345-369.

Pugh SD, Dietz J, Brief AP and Wiley JW (2008). Looking inside and out: The impact of employee and community demographic composition on organizational diversity climate. *Journal of Applied Psychology* 93 (6): 1422-1428.

Rachman, G. 2015. Paris attacks: the global consequences. Financial Times. 14th November 2015. Retrieved from: http://www.ft.com/cms/s/2/7b201298-8ab1-11e5-a549-b89a1dfede9b.html#axzz3tuM43aDE (accessed: 10 March 2016)

Risberg, A., & Søderberg, A. M. 2008. Translating a management concept: Diversity management in Denmark. *Gender Management: An International Journal*, 23(6): 426-441.

Robinson, D., and Spiegel, P. 2015. EU ministers force through refugee quota plan. Financial Times. 22nd September 2015. Retrieved from: http://www.ft.com/intl/cms/s/0/76c2dd9e-6111-11e5-9846-de406ccb37f2.html#axzz3tuM43aDE (accessed: 10 March 2016)

Rolandsen Agustin, L. 2011. *The policy on gender equality in Denmark*: European Parliament.

Rose, C. 2007. Does female board representation influence firm performance? The Danish evidence. *Corporate Governance*, 15(2): 404-413.

Schramm-Nielsen, J. 2001. Cultural Dimensions of Decision-Making: Denmark and France compared. Journal of Managerial Psychology, 16 (6): 404-423.

Syed J. and Ozbligin M, (2009), "A relational framework for international transfer of diversity management practices", *International Journal of Human Resource Management*, 20, (12),159-77.

Tatli, A. 2010. *Towards an integrated relational theory of diversity management*. Paper presented at the Academy of Management, Montreal.

Tatli, A. 2011. A multi-layered exploration of the diversity management field: Diversity discourses, practices and practitioners in the UK. British Journal of Management, 22, 238-253.

Tatli, A., Vassilopoulou, J., Al Ariss, A., & Özbilgin, M. 2012. The role of regulatory and temporal context in the construction of diversity discourses: The Case of the UK, France and Germany. *European Journal of Industrial Relations*.

Vermeulen, P. J. 2011. Diversity management in higher education: A South African perspective in comparison to a homogeneous and monomorphous society such as Germany: Center for Higher Education Development, Gütersloh.

Wrench, J. 2002. *Diversity management, discrimination and ethnic minorities in Europe: Clarifications, critiques and research agendas*. Linköping: Centre for Ethnic and Urban Studies.

3 SELF-INITIATION EXPATRIATION AS A NEW TREND IN INTERNATIONAL HRM

Sylwia Przytula

TABLE OF CONTENTS

Abstract

The globalized world economy demand increasing global mobility and flexibility in the workplace and workforce. There are various mobile employees in the international context [OECD] among which are self-initiated expatriates (SIEs). SIEs are now not only the most frequently employed staff by international employers, but also constitute "an alternative model of international careers". In the world literature self-initiated expatriation issues already lays claim to the status of a new sub-discipline in HRM, due to the growing interest in this specific group of international employees and otherness in their management. The purpose of this chapter is to present this new and emerging trend of SIE and allocate it in the context of IHRM.

Mail contact: s_przytula@wp.pl

1   Globalization as the key challenge for multinational corporations (MNCs)

Globalization with its main mechanisms being new information and communication technologies and cheap travels by air became a generally accepted construct, a buzzword used in debates concerning international mobility (Castles & Miller, 2009). The globalized world economy demand increasing global mobility and flexibility (Przytuła, 2013) in the workplace and workforce. There are many stakeholders on the global economic scene, of which the multinational corporations (MNCs) are the most important and powerful because they significantly influence the economy of their home and host countries (Dunning & Lundan, 2008; Rugmann, 2010).

Pursuant to the World Investment Report (UNTCAD, 2009), the number of corporations and their subsidiaries throughout the world has increased almost twice for a decade. Also, and the number of people employed in foreign subsidiaries of multinational corporations increased from 25 million in 1990 to 73 million in 2006. Multinational corporations are multicultural organizations with more than one national culture followed and represented by the personnel employed there, which influences the diversity of their world views, life styles, mental models, social skills or language, and is manifested in the behaviors of its stakeholders (Rozkwitalska & Sułkowski, 2016). The employees of multinational companies identify the key challenges in their jobs which include mainly cultural differences and multilingualism (Lauring & Selmer, 2011) and global mobility (Economist Intelligence Unit Survey, 2010). Thus, multicultural teams will be the norm rather than exception and diversity across countries be much more significant in managing human resources.

2   Migration and expatriation

Migration can be defined as physical movement from one geographical point to another one (Agozino, 2000), crossing national borders. Migration have been present from the very beginning although their intensity and forms have been different over the centuries and people have migrated for different reasons (for business purposes, sightseeing and satisfying cognitive curiosity, travel, to escape war, etc.)

Pursuant to the International Organization for Migration, (IOM, 2014), the number of migrants in the world equals 241 million, which constitutes 3% of the world population. In the years 1990-2013, the number of international migrants increased by 50%, that is by 77 million people. Thus, the migrants may form the fifth country in the world in terms of the size of its population (Gadkowski, 2010).

While skilled professionals are only a small segment of the 3% of the internationally mobile labor force-it is about one-fifth of international migrants who are highly skilled (International Organization for Migration (IOM), 2015). According to Ewers (2007), they are called "key engines" of the global knowledge economy or sometimes as the "best and brightest" (Batalova & Lowell, 2007) and "pool of talents" (Vaiman et al., 2015).

At present, the strategic challenge for multinational corporations includes staffing, development, and motivation of employees who are able to work in multicultural teams worldwide (McDonnel et al., 2010). However, the expatriation is not a result of growing demand for global specialists with multinational experience or is not the result of satisfying the expats' individual needs in the scope of development (acquiring better experience in working abroad to increase their employability in the future, Farndale et al., 2010). It is rather the result of competition between corporations for employing, attracting those "scarce" resources of highly qualified employees who can ensure international success for a corporation. The worldwide demand for human talents seems limitless with well-educated people transferring between countries and contributing to the world economy (Beaverstock, 2005). In PwC annual survey of CEOs (Dealing with Disruption, 2013) from around the world on what worries them most, 58% of the respondents expressed concerns about talent deficit. Similarly, in 2013 survey by Ernst & Young (Business Pulse, 2013) of companies across industries in 21 countries, the respondents identified the shortage of talent as among the top ten risks confronting their organizations.

Thus, the recruitment of highly qualified multinational employees is a key and strategic challenge for such entities. The research by Edstrom & Galbright (1977), expanded by Bartlett & Ghosal (1989) and Dowling & Festing (2008), show that multinational corporations use the services provided by expatriates to fulfil three motives: to bridge the gap in qualifications in the local market, to ensure the managers' development through their multinational experience, and to control and coordinate the activities carried out in the local market.

Other reasons are such that expats ensure the transfer of corporate culture, transfer of *know-how* (Brookfield, 2015), enable building of corporate knowledge platforms related to the specificity of local markets (Przytuła, 2014), develop interpersonal communication channels (network builders), improve the command of foreign languages (language node) (Dowling & Festing, 2008).

3   Assigned expatriation (AE) vs. self-initiated expatriation (SIE)

Thera are various mobile employees in the international context among which are migrant workers, organizational expatriates (OE) and self-initiated expatriates (SIE).

According to UN, migrant is "any person who changes his or her country of usual residence with the 'country of usual residence' representing the place where the person has the center of his life. While IOM defines a migrant as any person who is moving or has moved across an international border or within a state away from his/her habitual place of residence, regardless of (1) the person's legal status; (2) whether the movement is voluntary or involuntary; (3) what the causes for the movement are; or (4) what the length of the stay is (IOM, 2015).

Traditional research on international workers has focused on organizational, corporate or assigned expatriates (AE), so called because they have been sponsored and assigned by their parent organizations to the foreign location. Assigned expatriate refers to the employees who are temporarily relocated by their organizations to another country to complete a specific task or accomplish an organizational goal (Bonache & Brewster, 2001; Shaffer et al.,2012) to differentiate them from those who are locally employed (and may also be foreigners).

Increasingly more often, an assigned expatriate (AE) is replaced by other forms of expatriation encompassing foreign assignments which are shorter, less costly, and more oriented to the completion of a specific project (Beaverstock, 2005). Non-standard assignments such as commuter, rotational, contractual, extended business travel, self-initiated expatriation remained relatively unexamined (Peiperl et al., 2014), and over 40% of the workforce will fall into the non-organizational employee category. Pursuant to the research by the Worldwide ERC, 61 % of surveyed companies expects the increase in the number of short-term contracts, and in the scope of a form of "business commuter" foreign assignments - as many as 70% of respondents expects their increase in European companies (Worldwide ERC, 2009). The data from longitudinal studies performed by Brookfield shows similar results, where - after the financial crisis in 2008 - corporations reduced the costs mainly through reducing the number of long-term contracts and their replacement with short-term contracts whose term is from 3 to 12 months (Brookfield, 2015). In table 1 the differences between AEs and SIEs were presented:

Table 1. Assigned vs. self-initiated expatriates

	Differentiating criteria	Assigned expatriate	Self-initiated expatriate
1	organizational affiliation	• employed by one corporation; • is obliged to take assignment suggested by the corporation;	• is not permanently associated with any organization; • can also work with several organizations;
2	organization of foreign mission and financial support	• a high level of support from the sending and the receiving unit (preparation, staying for expat and his family, return and support on matters not related to their professional work is ensured by the corporation and a subsidiary) • costs related to relocation covers the sending and/or receiving organization	• independently organizing the trip (usually without the involvement of family members); • no support from the host organization on matters unrelated to work; • private funds for relocation
3	intended period of staying abroad	• limited-working for a subsidiary corporation for the time specified in the contract, • usually they are, once or repeatedly trips lasting from 1-5 years;	• unlimited- length of stay abroad depends on the duration of the project or task, but also on individual plans and decisions of SIE; • missions are frequent, but brief;
4	motives of going abroad	• organizational motives are predominant (filling in the staffing gaps in the local market; control and coordination of the activities of subsidiaries abroad) • economic (improvement of living standard, financial situation); • non-economic (related to internal development) – the expats derive satisfaction from their work abroad and consider it an important stage in their personal development • family issues	• individual and personal motives are predominant (travel, adventure, lifestyle change, escape from the problems) • work abroad is a voluntary choice of the so-called "voluntary displacement", • building own career paths *(boundary less career)* • increasing his/her market value and employability as a result of the acquired unique knowledge, experience, and interpersonal relations *(networking)*

	Differentia-ting criteria	Assigned expatriate	Self-initiated expatriate
5	socio-cultural adaptation and perception in host countries	• life in expats' enclaves, poor integration with the local staff and inhabitants due to the feeling of "temporariness" • rather positive perception	• greater than in AEs case the ability to integrate with the local community, • better understanding of local culture and easier adaptation • preparation to live and work in a foreign country and culture on his/her own • rather positive perception
6	direction of transfer	• crossing national but not organizational boundaries • from developing countries to developed countries; however, the prevailing direction is from developed countries (where headquarters are usually located) to emerging markets (prospective, yet problematic destinations)	• crossing national and organizational boundaries • SIEs display higher than expatriates organizational mobility and intention to change organization
7	level of assurance, safety and job satisfaction	• job security during the term of the contract, • no organizational solutions for repatriates in terms of jobs and place in the corporate structure makes them leave the organization • wide range of financial incentives, various forms of economic support for families, high level of satisfaction from work	• reliability and job safety depend on the SIE-alone decides about having a job or finished contract • job satisfaction very high

Source: Doherty et al, 2011; Selmer & Lauring, 2010; Sargent, 2002; Biemann et al, 2010; Al Ariss, 2010; Castles & Miller, 2011; Przytuła, 2015.

Contemporary SIEs are diverse group such as seekers (Inkson & Myers, 2003), young graduates (Tharenou, 2003), English teachers (Fu et al., 2005), academics (Isakovic et al., 2013; Richardson & McKenna,2006), volunteer workers (Hudson, Inkson, 2006), nurses (Bozionelos, 2009), doctors (Nolan & Morley, 2014) and business professionals (Fitzgerald, 2008; Jokinen, et al., 2008; Lee, 2005). There is no standard definition of the term "self-initiated expatriates" but researchers stress the need for such a standard (Doherty, 2013).

Inkson et al. (1997) introduced category of "self- initiated foreign work experience- SFE" which was developed by Suutari & Brewster (2000), also "self-selecting expatriates" (Richardson & McKenna, 2003), "self-initiated movers" (Thorn, 2009), "self-designed apprenticeship" (Arthur et al., 1999), "free travelers" (Myers & Pringle, 2005) but the nomenclature SFE has converged to the widely accepted "SIE" category of international assignee (Al Ariss & Crowley-Henry, 2013).

SIEs are individuals who personally take responsibility of their careers without the direct support of an organization (Carr et al., 2005). SIE are professionals who choose to expatriate and who are not transferred by their employer (Harrison et al., 2004), they relocate to a country of their choice to seek a job or to try an entrepreneurial venture (Jokinen et al., 2008; Saxenian, 2005). So SIEs initiate their own expatriation than are assigned by their company, as shown from professionals from Western countries (65% self-initiated expatriates vs. 35% assigned expatriates, Doherty, 2013).

Tharenou (2013) conceptualizes SIEs as corporate, managerial expatriates on the basis that they "independently cross both country and organizational boundaries to seek work in a new organization which recruits them from the local labor market".

McNulty proposes the various sub-types of SIEs include: foreign executives in local organization (FELOs); local foreign hires (LFHs); expat-preneurs, self-initiated corporate expatriates (SICEs) and third country nationals (TCNs) (McNulty & DeCieri, 2015).

4   Self-initiated expatriation' implications for HRM

Although the management of expatriation is accorded significant status in the international human resource management literature, since it is seen as a key contributor to firm performance, it appears that expatriate management remains a weakness for many organizations (Shaffer et al., 2012) and is often somewhat separated from the organization's global policy of HRM. More than three decades of research and progress in the field related to expatriation management have not succeeded in making expatriation management an integrated element of strategic human resource management (Cerdin & Brewster, 2014). The more, new stream of expatriate management such as SIE causes considerable confusion for IHRM.

SIEs are now not only the most frequently employed staff by international employers, but also constitute "an alternative model of international careers" (Myers & Pringle, 2005). Other researchers (Jokinen et al., 2008) indicate that this "hidden aspect of the international labor market", which demonstrates little understanding and minimal information about them in scientific publications, and official statistics on a global scale. In the world literature self-initiated expatriation issues already lays claim to the status of a new sub-discipline in HRM (Andresen et al., 2013; Howe-Walsh & Schyns, 2010; Suutari & Brewster, 2000), due to the growing interest in this specific group of international employees and otherness in their management.

Another significant topic is a parallel discussion concerning the issue of qualified migrants (their demographic profile, change in professional preferences, the directions and reasons for relocations, growing number of women-migrants).These issues mainly took place in social sciences (sociology, demography, political sciences), but country-comparative work on the topic of the management of international migrants (as a source of global talent and competitiveness to organization) is clearly missing. We don't know how national HRM practices differ in their selection, recruitment, training and development, retention of international migrants (Al Ariss, 2016).

In view of the diversity of needs, motives and attitudes presented by the new group of internationally mobile employees, the HR practitioners, scientists, researchers and policy makers need to examine how traditional employment practices and concepts-such as performance appraisal, turnover, absenteeism, organizational commitment, leadership and so on-have to be revised in the light of these new realities (Tung, 2016).

Below, selected areas of HRM were presented, which noted significant differences in the ways of managing AEs and SIEs.

Recruitment and selection. The selection criteria have been the subject of a large body of literature, with emphasis placed on criteria such as partner support and communication skills. Moreover, the focus on technical skills found in the early research has persisted (Andreson, 2005) and indeed the process by which employees are selected for expatriation is often not as formalized as one might expect (Harris & Brewster, 1999).

Local subsidiaries should maintain regular ties with various local networking organizations (e.g. Chamber of Commerce) for attracting SIE who make in this way connections leading to possible employment opportunities. Social networking resources such as special interest groups on LinkedIn and especially expatriate-focused sites such as InterNations, Expatica, ExpatForum, ExpatFocus can be helpful in identifying local SIE (Vaiman & Brewster,2014).

The competence profile also differs from the traditionally accepted one where candidate's experience and knowledge were key requirements for candidates for foreign assignments (Przytuła, 2014). In the case of SIEs, we deal with a different psychological contract than in the case of AEs. The decisions concerning the work abroad made by SIEs are characterized by transactional contracts, while the traditional expats combine foreign assignments also with the development of network of links and social relations, which is typical of relational contracts (Coyle-Shapiro et al., 2008). The level of commitment to work and loyalty towards the employing organizations in SIEs is also different. It results from short-term contracts in comparison to the case of the employees connected with the company for many years, prepared for the assignment, trained, paid, who can rely on the support of the home undertaking also during their assignment.

Cultural training is complimentary to the recruitment and selection process in the sense that it enables the organization to evaluate and confirm further the candidates' aptitude for expatriation and even to take into consideration their families (Halserberger & Brewster, 2008). Research shows that multinational corporations don't implement cultural training extensively in their expatriation policy. 83% of AEs acknowledged that they did not participate in cross-cultural training (Brookfield). On the other hand, research findings of Przytuła (2014) proved that 73% of responded expatriates had problems in their daily work connected with cultural differences. Lack of preparation and conduct of intercultural training for expatriates is because the link between such training and expatriate performance remains hard to confirm (Puck et al., 2008).

Career development. The model of career of assigned expatriates and SIE are often characterized by the concepts of traditional and boundary less careers. New concepts of protean and boundary less career (Altman & Baruch, 2012) emphasized the individual intentionality in shaping of career and blurring of organization boundaries which have thus far constituted the frameworks of employees' careers. But Andresen et al. (2015) argued that career concepts are likely to differ between AE and SIE. It is about the evolution of a path of global career for the last three decades. In the 1990s, the characteristic expatriation path was motivated with development of career, while since 2000 the model of path of the career motivated with personal development has become clearly noticeable (Altman & Baruch, 2012). Thus, the expatriation is motivated in two ways: development of own career or personal development. In the first case, it is about the development of knowledge and social capital (network of individual contacts). In the case of the career focused on personal development, it is about the creation of internal capital (self-confidence, self-awareness and self-efficiency) and of cultural capital (Altman & Baruch 2012). Given the aforementioned, it is possible to distinguish the following types of global careers: global careers being the result of individual migration, assigned careers (typical of traditional expatriates who fulfil foreign assignments in connection with the objectives of the organization), individual careers (typical of SIEs who pursue their own vision of development (Miś, 2016).

Those different models determine the activities undertaken within the personnel function in the area of employees' development and qualification improvement. After their return from the assignment, assigned expatriates (AEs) may rely on traditional career with its classical structural development which should be ensured by the home undertaking. The studies by Brookfield in that scope prove that the expatriate's experience influences faster promotion and easier access to higher positions in corporate structures (it is stated by about 38% of expatriates involved in the study). In the case of SIEs, the plan of career formed individually is focused on the development of employability. It is so because for SIEs, the expatriation is not a goal itself but rather a result of their efforts to achieve other objectives.

Motivation. The process of motivational activities undertaken by the company should refer to individual motives and employee's needs - yet, they differ in both groups of expatriates. The international studies show that the most frequent reasons for decisions concerning foreign assignments for assigned expatriates (AEs) are the issues connected with professional career (development of skills and abilities, professional challenges while working abroad), the issues of personal relations and family issues (safety, family benefits), financial incentives. Further motives include cognitive ones (to see and explore the world, to live an adventure, the willingness to live in the host country). In the case of SIEs, the motives for making the decisions are slightly different, and the most frequently listed ones include travelling (to live an adventure, to explore the world, the willingness to live in the host country), professional career (new professional challenges, new projects) (Doherty et al., 2013). While in the studies by Cerdin (2013), no significant differences in the motives for undertaking foreign assignments by SIEs and OEs are noticeable.

For both group of expats personal challenge, professional development and importance of the job itself, were equally high in the rankings, although in a different order. The three first motivation factors are in order of importance for SIEs: 1) personal challenge, 2) professional development, 3) importance of the job itself. For AEs the most important was: 1) professional development, 2) importance of the job itself, 3) personal challenge.

In spite of some small differences that resulted from such studies, a corporation employing both groups of employees should offer them different approach to motivation and development. In relation to SIEs, the organization should emphasize the fulfilment of needs in the scope of development and present challenges at work, as well as promote the idea of work-life balance as such are the priority motives for SIEs (Cerdin, 2013).

Repatriation management remains an organizational weakness in international mobility (Kraimer et al, 2009; Lazarova & Cerdin, 2007). Although the expatriation is nearly always a success for those individuals who went abroad (95% of foreign mission end up with success, Brookfield, 2015), they often leave the corporation upon return (25% of repatriates leave the company within 2 years after return to home country).

In the case of SIEs, there is no stage of repatriation from the organization's point of view as an expat does not return to the organization (the headquarters) that has sent them. The benefits from the assignment are thus obtained by the expatriates themselves in a form of gained knowledge and multinational experience, establishment of contacts and relations with local stakeholders (networking), the feeling of satisfaction and self-fulfillment, increased self-esteem (Przytuła, 2014). It enables the expats to increase their value and employability in the global labor market, negotiate new contracts taking into account the aforementioned new experience and qualifications.

5   Final remarks

The grounds for competitive advantage of MNCs include at present highly qualified, mobile, flexible multinational employees with the command of foreign languages who - in spite of being a small number in terms of global migrations - are a crucial source of competitive advantage of MNCs. On the one hand, the multicultural character of human resources is a demographic feature of corporate employees (Arasaratnam, 2013), on the other hand, a unique characteristic of MNCs (Rozkwitalska & Sułkowski, 2016).

A special challenge for the HRM is a new population of the so-called self-initiated expatriates (SIEs). Although the literature on the subject concerning different sub-functions of the HRM (recruitment, selection, motivation, adjustment, career development, repatriation) is very extensive, it is still somehow left out during the discussions within the IHRM and is sometimes inconsistent with the assumptions of the global personnel strategy adopted in a corporation. Furthermore, a different nature of managing the new group of SIEs who will dominate foreign assignments in the future requires that the HRM is redefined because the strategies and methods effective thus far in the management of AEs are completely ineffective in relation to SIEs.

As the global shortage of highly-skilled workers is increasing, the need for attracting and keeping self-initiated expats seems to be predominant for global companies.

Thus, we have to deal with the necessity of ordering and redefining numerous HRM areas in the scope of theory development (defining the term of 'SIE', specifying the profile of personality and competence), and in the empirical area - with the necessity of developing the tools supporting the effective management of such employees, that is the tools aimed at their attraction, selection, adaptation, motivation, career development and retention. It can be stated that the IHRM is *in statu nascendi* in relation to SIEs.

References:

Al Ariss, A., & Crowley-Henry, M. (2013). Self-initiated expatriation and migration in the management literature: Present theorizations and future research directions. *Career Development International*, *18*(1), 78–96.

Altman, Y., Baruch, Y. (2012). Global protean careers:a new era in expatriation and repatriation. *Personnel Review*, *41*(2).

Andresen, M., AlAriss, A., Walther, M. (2013). Introduction:Self-Initiated Expatriation-Individual, Organizational and National Perspectives. In M. Andresen, M., Al Ariss, A., Walther (Ed.), *Self-Initiated Expatriation.Individual, Organizational, and National Perspectives* (pp. 3–10). New York, London: Routledge.

Andresen, M., Biemann, T., Pattie, M. (2015). What makes them move abroad?Reviewing and exploring differences between self-initiated and assigned expatriation. *International Journal of Human Resource Management, forthcomin.*

Andreson, B. (2005). Expatriate selcetion:good management or good luck? *International of Human Resource Management*, *16*(4), 567–583.

Arasaratnam, L. A. (2013). A review of articles on multiculturalism in 35 years of IJIR. *International Journal of Intercultural Relations*, *37*(6), 676–685.

Arthur, M.B., Inkson, K., Pringle, J. K. (1999). *The New Careers:individual action and economic change*. (P. J. K. Arthur MB., Inkson K., Ed.). London: Sage Publications.

Bartlett, C, Ghosal, S. (1989). *Managing across borders: the trasnational solution*. Cambridge, MA: Harvard Business School Press.

Batalova, J., Lowell, L. (2007). Immigrant professionals in the United States. *Society*, *44*(2), 26–31.

Beaverstock, J. V. (2005). Transnational elites in the city: British highly-skilled inter-company transferees in New York City's financial district'. *Journal of Ethnic and Migration Studies*, *31*(2), 245–268.

Bonache, J., & Brewster, C. (2001). Knowledge transfer and the management of expatriation. *Thunderbird International Business Review*, *43*(1), 145–168.

Bozionelos, N. (2009). Expatriation outside the boundaries of the multinational corporation: a study with expatriate nurses in Saudi Arabia. *Human Resource Management*, *48*(1), 111–134.

Brookfield Global Relocation Trends. (2015). *Global Mobility Trends Survey*. New York.

Carr, S. C., Inkson, K., Thorn, K. J. (2005). From global careers to talent flow: Re-interpreting brain drain. *Journal of World Business*, *40*, 386–398.

Castles, S., Miller, M. (2009). *The age of migration.International population movements in the modern world*. Palgrave Macmillan.

Cerdin, J.L., Brewster, C. (2014). Talent management and expatriation:bridging two streams of research and practice. *Journal of World Business*, *49*, 245–252.

Cerdin, J. L. (2013). Motivation of self-initiated expatriates. In M. Andresen, M., AlAriss, A., Walther (Ed.), *Self-initiated expatriation.Individual, organizational and national perspectives*. New York: Routledge.

Coyle-Shapiro, Jacqueline A., Parzefall, M. (2008). Psychological contracts. In J. Cooper, L. Barling (Ed.), *The SAGE handbook of organizational behavior* (pp. 17–34). London: Sage Publications.

Doherty, N. (2013). Understanding the self-initiated expatriate: A review and directions for future research. *International Journal of Management Reviews*, *15*(4), 447–469. http://doi.org/10.1111/ijmr.12005

Doherty, N., Richardson, J., & Thorn, K. (2013). Self-initiated expatriation: Career experiences, processes and outcomes. *Career Development International*, *18*(1), 6–11. http://doi.org/10.1108/13620431311305917

Dowling P., Festing M., E. A. (2008). *International Human Resource Management*. South-Western Cengage Learning.

Dunning, J.H., Lundan, S. M. (2008). *Multinational enterprises and the global economy* (2nd ed.). Edward Elgar Publishing.

Economist Intelligence Unit Survey. (2010). *Global firms in 2020.The next decade of change for organization and workers*.

Edstörm A., Galbright, J. R. (1977). Transfer of managers as a coordination and control strategy in multinational organizations. *Administrative Science Quarterly*, *22*(2), 248–263.

Ewers, M. (2007). Migrants, markets and multinationals:competition among world cities for the highly skilled. *GeoJournal*, *68*(2-3), 119–130.

Farndale, E., Scullion, H., Sparrow, P. (2010). The role of the corporate HR function in global talent mangement. *Journal of World Business*, *45*(2), 161–168.

Fitzgerald, C., Howe-Walsh, L. (2008). Self-initiated expatriates:an interpretative phenomenological analysis of professional female expatriates. *International Journal of Business Mangement*, *3*(10), 156–175.

Fu,C.K., Shaffer, M., Harrison, D. A. (2005). *Proactive socialization, adjustment and turnover:a study of self-initiated foreign employyes*.

Gadkowski, T. (2010). Problematyka ochrony migrantów w międzynarodowym prawie praw człowieka. In K. Ilski (Ed.), *Obrazy migracji*. Poznań: Instytut Historii UAM.

Harris, H., Brewster, C. (1999). The coffee-machine system:how international selection really works? *International of Human Resource Management*, *10*(3), 488–500.

Harrison, D.A., Shaffer, M.A., Bhaskar-Shrinivas, P. (2004). Going places: Roads more or less traveled in research on expatriate experiences'. In J.J.Martochio (Ed.), *Research in personnel and human resources management*.

Howe-Walsh, L., & Schyns, B. (2010). Self-initiated expatriation : implications for HRM. *International Journal of Human Resource Management*, *21*(2), 260–273. http://doi.org/10.1080/09585190903509571

Hudson, S., Inkson, K. (2006). Volunteer overseas development workers:The heroes' adventure and personal transformation. *Career Development International*, *11*(4), 304–320.

Inkson, K., & Myers, B. (2003). The big OE: Self-directed travel and career development. *Career Development International*, *8*, 170–181.

Inkson, K., Arthur, M.B., Pringle, J., Barry, S. (1997). Expatriate Assignment versus Overseas Experience:International Human Resource Development. *Journal of World Business*, *32*, 351–368.

International Organization for Migration (IOM). (2015). *World Migration 2015*. Geneva.

Isakovic, A.A., Whitman, M. (2013). Self-initoiated expatriate adjustment in the United Arab Emirates:a study of academics. *Journal of Global Mobility*, *1*(2), 161–186.

Jokinen, T., Brewster, C., Suutari, V. (2008). Career capital during international work experiences:contrasting self-initiated expatriate experiences and assigned expatriation. *The International Journal of Human Resource Management*, *19*(6), 979–998.

Kraimer, M., Shaffer, M., Bolino, M. (2009). The influence of expatriate and repatriate experiences on career advencement and repatriate retention. *Human Resource Management*, *48*(1), 22–47.

Lauring, J., & Selmer, J. (2011). Multicultural organizations: common language, knowledge sharing and performance. *Personnel Review*, *40*(3), 324–343.

Lazarova, M., Cerdin, J. L. (2007). Revisiting repatriation concerns:organizational support vs. career and contextual influences. *Journal of International Business Studies*, *38*(3), 404–429.

Lee, C. H. (2005). A study of underemployment among self-initiated expatriates. *Journal of World Business*, *40*, 172–187.

McDonnel, A., Lamare, R., Gunnigle, P., Lavelle, J. (2010). Developing tomorrow's leaders:evidence of global talent management in multinational enterprises. *Journal of World Business*, *45*(2), 150–160.

McNulty, I., DeCieri, H. (2015). Linking global mobility and global talent management:the role of ROI. *Employee Relations*, *38*(1), 8–30.

Mellahi, K., Collings, D. (2010). The barriers to effective global talent management:the example of corporate elites in MNEs. *Journal of World Business*, *45*(2), 143–149.

Miś, A. (2016). Kariery ponad granicami. In A. Pocztowski (Ed.), *Zarzadzanie zasobami ludzkimi na rynkach międzynarodowych*. Warszawa: Wolters Kluwer Polska.

Myers, B., Pringle, J. K. (2005). Self-initiated foreign experience as accelerated development:influences of gender. *Journal of World Business*, *40*, 421–431.

Nolan, E.M., Morley, M. (2014). A test of the relationship between person–environment fit and cross-cultural adjustment among self-initiated expatriates. *International Journal of Human Resource Management*, *25*(11), 1631–1649.

Peiperl, M.Levy, O., Sorell, M. (2014). Cross border mobility of self-initiated and organizational expatriates. *International Studies of Management and Organization*, *44*(3), 44–65.

Przytuła, S. (2013). Flexibility - as a feature and the ability in the expatriate' qualification profile. *Education of Economists and Managers*, *27*, 51–65.

Przytuła, S. (2014). *Zarządzanie kadrą ekspatriantów w filiach przedsiębiorstw międzynarodowych w Polsce*. Warszawa: CeDeWu.

Przytuła, S. (2015). Migrants, Assigned Expatriates (AE) and Self-initiated Expatriates (SIE) - Dfferentiation of Terms and Literature-Based Research Review. *Journal of Intercultural Management*, *7*(2), 89–112.

Puck, J., Kittler, M., Wright, C. (2008). Doe it really work?Re-assessing the impact of pre-departure cross-cultural training on expatriate adjustment. *International Journal of Human Resource Management*, *19*(12), 2182–2197.

Richardson, J., McKenna, S. (2006). Exploring relationship with home and host countries:a study of self-directed expatriates. *Cross Cultural Management*, *13*(1), 6–22.

Richardson, J., McKenna, S. (2003). International Experience and Academic Careers. What Do Academics Have to Say? *Personnel Review*, *32*(6), 774–795.

Rozkwitalska, M., Sułkowski, Ł. (Ed.). (2016). *Współpraca zawodowa w środowisku wielokulturowym*. Warszawa: Wolters Kluwer Polska.

Rugmann, A. M. (Ed.). (2010). *The Oxford Handbook of International Business* (2nd ed.). New York: Oxford University Press.

Saxenian, A. (2005). From brain drain to brain circulation. *Studies in Comparative International Development*, *40*(2), 35–61.

Shaffer, M., Kraimer, M., Chen, Y., Bollino, M. . (2012). Choices , challenges and career consequences of global work experience:a review for future agenda. *Journal of Management*, *38*.

Suutari, V., Brewster, C. (2000). Making their own way:international experience through self-initiated foreign assignments. *Journal of World Business*, *35*(4), 417–436.

Tharenou, P. (2003). The initial development of receptivity to working abroad: Self-initiated international work opportunities in young graduate employees. *Journal of Occupational and Organizational Psychology*, *76*, 489–515.

Tharenou, P. (2013). Self-initiated expatriate:an alternative to company assigned expatriates? *Journal of Global Mobility*, *1*(3), 336–356.

Thorn, K. (2009). The relative importance of motives for international self-initiated mobility. *Career Development International*, *14*(5), 441–464.

Tung, R. (2016). New perspectives on human resource management in a global context. *Journal of World Business*, *51*, 142–152.

UNTCAD. (2009). *World Investment Report.Overview*.

Vaiman, V., Haslberger, A., Vance, C. (2015). Recognizing the important role of self-initiated expatriates in effective global talent management. *Human Resource Management Review*, *25*, 280–286.

Worldwide ERC. (2009). *Global Benchmarking Survey*.

4 EMPLOYEE DEVELOPMENT WITHIN EUROPEAN SOCIAL FUND IN POLAND: PRELIMINARY RESEARCH FINDINGS

Katarzyna Tracz-Krupa

TABLE OF CONTENTS

Abstract

The goal of the article is to present initial empirical studies concerning employee development in SMEs on the basis of European Social Fund (ESF) in Poland in the perspective of 2007-2013. The empirical studies were carried out in 50 SME in 2016 in Opole and Lower Silesia Region, using CATI method. Conclusions in the final research relate to the reasons for applying for EU projects, types of training and development activities as well as plans regarding EU perspective of 2014-2020.

Mail contact: katarzyna.tracz@ue.wroc.pl

1   Introduction

For over than a decade Poland has noted a growing interest in obtaining EU funds on training and development activities. Study named *Human Capital* conducted by the Polish Agency for Enterprise Development in cooperation with Jagiellonian University indicated that every seventh entrepreneur in Poland took advantage of the European Social Fund (ESF) in reference to employee development (PARP, 2013).

The article focuses on employee development of micro, small and medium-sized enterprises (SMEs), resulting from European Social Fund grants in Poland in the years 2007-2013. The major reason for undertaking this research is lack of empirical studies on the topic in Poland. There is a scant number of publications on the benefits of ESF grants for development of employees' qualifications in Polish organizations. In the second EU financial perspective, 2007-2013, Poland received 11 429 billion Euro, thus becoming the biggest beneficiary of the EU funds among all new member states. By the end of 2014 more than 355,5 thousand enterprises benefited with support for the development activities in Poland (Ministry of Infrastructure and Development, 2016). In the subject literature there are no qualitative data regarding the objectives, types and effects of training activities financed by EU funds. There are only ministerial reports available of a rather descriptive nature; they do not include explicative and predictive perspective (Tracz-Krupa, 2014).

Considering the above mentioned the purpose of this article is to bring forth the answers to the following research questions: What were the reasons underlying application of the ESF grants by the SMEs? Which training and development activities were financed by the ESF? Was the level of effectiveness of these activities evaluated? What were the results of the acquired funding? What were the obstacles the beneficiaries met at the stage of planning, organizing and supervision? Are the SMEs that previously obtained funding interested in applying again in the current financial perspective 2014-2020? These questions were asked at the stage of preliminary empirical research, which was conducted among the group of 50 enterprises in the SME sector.

The scheme of the article was adjusted properly to meet the above stated objective. The introductory part of the article covers the semantic scope of basic concepts used in the paper. The following part includes review of the conducted studies in the subject of employee development in SMEs. Later part of the paper presents the method and results of the author's own study. Finally, there are outlined conclusions of the study and recommendations for further exploration.

2 Theoretical background of employee development in the sector of SMEs and the concept of ESF

For clarity of considerations undertaken in this article it is necessary to explain key concepts such as employee development, sector of small and medium-sized enterprises and the European Social Fund. Referring to the first of these terms it is worth noting that there are many various definitions in the subject literature, yet they have more common features than differentiating ones.

Since the purpose of the article is not to bring it into a discussion, solely the definition of Listwan (1995) adopted in this study will be presented. Therefore, it is assumed that the employee development means the activities aimed at preparing employees to work and occupy positions of greater responsibility (Listwan, 1995). According to the organized action cycle it covers three phases:

- preparation, including the definition of objectives and the development plan for the employee,

- implementation, defining the activities related to the execution of employee development: training, transfer of employees and fulfillment in the workplace,

- supervision phase, including monitoring of development progress and revision of plans and development activities.

The dynamics and direction of employee development are determined on one hand by the goals of a company and on the other hand by the needs and aspirations of employees (Suchodolski, 2010).

Another issue of interest in this work is the sector of small and medium-sized enterprises (SME). The classification criteria for small and medium companies are differentiated in various countries, whereas the most common distinctive features are the level of employment and turnover. In Poland these criteria were defined in the Act on freedom of economic activity of 2 July 2004, which conformed to the guidelines issued by the European Commission on 6 March 2003. The Act defines three categories of enterprises:

- micro-enterprises, hiring fewer than 10 employees, with an annual turnover not exceeding 2 million EUR or of a total annual balance sheet not exceeding 2 million EUR;

- small enterprises employing fewer than 50 people, with an annual turnover not exceeding 10 million EUR or of a total annual balance sheet not exceeding 10 million EUR;

- medium-sized enterprises, employing fewer than 250 people, with an annual turnover not exceeding 50 million EUR or of an annual balance sheet not exceeding 43 million EUR.

Determinants of employee development in the sector of small and medium-sized (SME) enterprises based on the empirical research will be presented in the following part of this article. However, for demonstration and explanation purpose the publication of U. Pauli is recommended. The author describes the impact of professionalization of training as well as factors that influence development of small and medium-sized enterprises (see Pauli, 2010).

The last concept to be defined is the European Social Fund. It is the first and most fundamental structural fund in the European Union, which was created in 1957. It was established to increase the chances of getting a job within the European countries by promoting employment and increasing labor mobility (Tracz-Krupa, 2014). The Fund aims at leading long-term activities. These activities are focused on investment in human capital which is linked to improvement of the competitiveness of the Euro regions and to an increase in entrepreneurship (Grewiński, 2001). It is an instrument of the modern employment policy and the development of human resources which contributes to the achievement of socio-economic cohesion (Tracz-Krupa, 2014). Poland joined the structures of the European Union on the 1st May 2004. Upon accession the country also became the beneficiary of financial assistance provided in the framework of the EU structural policy using the EU funds. In the financial perspective 2007-2013 Poland became the largest beneficiary of the EU funds among all the member states receiving 68 billion Euro. Research on the use of these funds in Poland will be discussed later in this article.

3   The issue of employee development in SMEs from the perspective of empirical research

Empirical research on the development of employees is mainly conducted in the management sciences. However, due to the interdisciplinary nature, these issues are of interest to other scientific disciplines, including: economics, education, psychology or sociology (Chalofsky 2007 for: Pocztowski, 2013). The literature on the subject describes a number of studies on employee development, which can be divided according to the following criteria:

- the size of organization;
- type of organization: public and private;
- the national context (Tracz-Krupa, 2015).

The attention of the author will be focused on the first criterion differentiating the studies which is the size of organization. Both public and private organizations are discussed in the further part of this subchapter. In the subject literature the research is conducted separately in both SMEs and large organizations.

4   Specifics of employee development in SMEs

There is a strong belief, that SMEs have their own characteristics and activities in the field of human resource management, including the area of development, different from those undertaken by large organizations (Tracz-Krupa, 2015). The studies of Hill

53

and Stewart proved that small and medium-sized organizations are characterized by a short-term perspective and spontaneity in the implementation of the policy of human resource development (1999). Informality and flexibility of development activities in the sector of SMEs were elaborately characterized in the studies of Gibb (1997), Storey (1994) and Chaston (1997). Other researchers, e.g. Lane (1994) or Westhead and Storey (1997) proved that training is not prevalent in small organizations. Hill and Stewart are of the opinion that training is designed to solve specific problems in an organization as opposed to improving workers' qualifications (1999). Extensive comparative study on e-learning in organizations by Brown, Murphy and Wade shows that 67% of large enterprises and only 20% SMEs ones use this form of education (2006).

According to studies in Polish organizations regarding SMEs sector, aimed at diagnosing the level of professionalization of human resources management only 37% of SMEs conduct analysis of training needs, 31% of companies provide training in a cyclical manner, and only 30% examine the effectiveness of training (Pocztowski, Pauli, 2013). More optimistic results concerning studies of labor market in Poland named *Study of Human Capital* present the Polish Agency for Enterprise Development in cooperation with Jagiellonian University. The research, conducted continuously since 2010, shows that in beginning year 85% of all small businesses and 77% of micro-enterprises delegated their employees to participate in trainings. In total, in the SME sector, this ratio reached almost 90% (Żukowska, 2012).

Based on the review of literature and numerous studies the following determinants of SME activities in the area of development were distinguished: informality, short-term perspective, focus on solving current problems, concentration on the development of specific skills and organizational knowledge and failure to organize the training in a professional manner (Trochimiuk, 2013).

5   Employee development within European Social Fund in Poland – pilot-research findings

The author has made attempts to implement a pilot research study on a group of 50 enterprises from the SME sector. The purpose of the study was to bring forth the answers to the following research questions: What were the reasons underlying application of the ESF grants by the SMEs? Which training and development activities were financed by the ESF? Was the level of effectiveness of these activities evaluated? What were the results of the acquired funding? What were the obstacles the beneficiaries met at the stage of planning, organizing and supervision? Are the SMEs that previously obtained funding interested in applying again in the current financial perspective 2014-2020? These questions were asked using CATI method, computer assisted telephone interview within a group of 50 SMEs from the province of Lower Silesia and Opole Region in Poland, of which 40% were micro enterprises, 34% small companies and 26% of medium-sized entities (see figure No. 1).

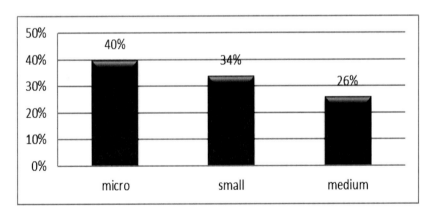

Figure 1: Structure of enterprises according to their size (Own research)

The group of enterprises selected for this study underwent purposive sampling. In the scope of interest were the businesses which obtained at least one funding from the ESF for training and development of employees. Size of an enterprise was taken into account. The selection of enterprises was thoroughly performed with regard to their size. Also their number was fairly equal. While creating the research group other criteria were considered. An important aspect was that the enterprises selected for the study were not homogenous. They were varied according to the industry and type of ownership. In the study both Polish and foreign enterprises were assessed. Altogether 50 interviews were conducted, one in each company, mainly with the managing staff. In most part, the interviewees could select a few possible answers. This is illustrated in the charts.

The research shows that the main reason for applying for funds from the ESF was the possibility to improve qualifications of employees (84% answers). Following that, 42% of respondents indicated possibility to decrease operational costs and 40% pointed to the increase in competitiveness of companies through offering higher quality of services. Other answers of the respondents included: possibility to improve competitive advantage (30%), capacity to decrease operational costs (14 %). 12% of the respondents declared that applying for EU funds is one of their main services. It should be noted that the respondents could choose more than one answer.

The study also helped to obtain data about the difficulties in applying for EU funds at the stage of planning, implementation and project supervision. 34% of the respondents declared that they did not encounter any difficulties, 32% claimed the process of application for the EU funds is too complicated. Other difficulties at the planning stage included overly long application process (26% of responses), insufficient qualifications and knowledge of clerks and high fees of consulting companies assisting in preparation of a grant application (16% responses).

The first step in a properly implemented procedure in training and development is identification of training needs. In the audited ESF projects 38% of managers requested training for their employees, 36% of employees indicated the training in which they were interested, 32% of organizations evaluated training needs once for the purpose of a EU project. Only 18% conducted training which was a part of an employee development plan, and only in 12% they resulted from employee interim evaluations.

84% of projects that were the subject of the study were directed to all employees, 28% to managers and senior executives and 20% to specialists (see figure No. 2).

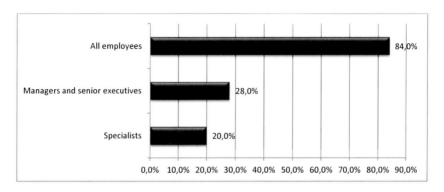

Figure 2: Beneficiaries of projects (Own research)

Gathered data show that computer training dominated in projects from the ESF (58% of respondents), followed by foreign language trainings (46%), interpersonal trainings (44%) and financial ones (22%). 54% of respondents marked another category which included the following trainings: managerial, legal, specific and industry (see figure No. 3).

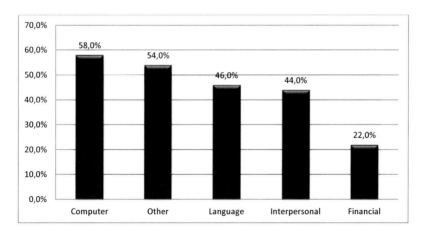

Figure 3: Types of training (Own research)

At the stage of implementation of ESF projects 52% of respondents indicated that they had no problems with the settlement of payment application. 28 % of beneficiaries pointed to an excessive meticulousness of clerks. 16% of companies had problems with recruitment and selection of the target group, and 12% indicated that the start of a project was delayed due to prolonged evaluation of proposals and the final signing of the contract. In addition, respondents answered that the value of some items in the budget was reduced, making it difficult to implement the project. There was lack of communication between institutions settling the EU projects at regional and central level and as a result, the funding from those institutions were delayed (see figure No. 4).

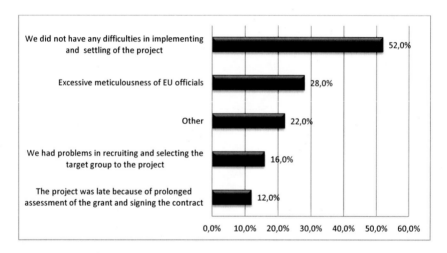

Figure No. 4. Difficulties related to the settlement of the grant application (own research)

During the interviews also information on evaluating the effectiveness of training activities by Kirkpatrick was collected. 72% of respondents declared that they evaluated the response, which is how the participants reacted to the training. Only 56% of enterprises assessed the effects of training in the learning phase, knowledge of the subject was checked. Only 36% of companies monitored the employee behavior, they observed whether there were any changes in workers' attitudes. None of the respondents referred to the fourth level of training effectiveness, which is evaluation of training results.

Collected data show that 90% respondents claimed increased employees' qualifications being a result of training. 62% of the beneficiaries were of an opinion that training influenced positively their competitive advantage, and 56% observed increased level of employee motivation and commitment. In addition, 36% of the respondents claimed they built an image of a good employer, and 32% stated they had financial benefits from implementation of projects (see figure No. 5).

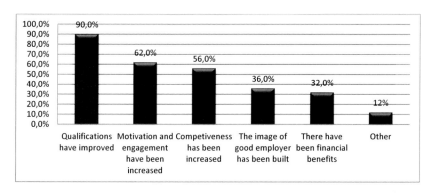

Figure 5: The effects of participation in the project (Own research)

The respondents were also asked whether the project would be carried out without EU co-financing. 38% of respondents gave a negative answer, 34% declared that it would be on a lower scale, and 24% were not able to give a response (see figure No. 6).

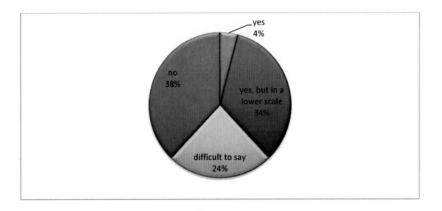

Figure 6: Implementation of project without EU funding (Own research)

These data in conjunction with the question of assessment of the financial and economic condition of the company may be surprising, since 84% of companies declared that it is good or very good (see figure No. 7). On this basis, it can be concluded that these companies do not treat investment in human capital as a priority because in most cases such actions have not been taken. However, they have the knowledge of how important human resource management is with regard to the functioning and competitive advantage of a business, in particular investment in employee development. This is because they were in a group of institutions which received EU funds for training and development activities.

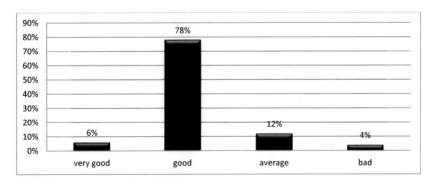

Figure 7: Assessment of financial and economic condition of an enterprise
(Own research)

In the study the respondents had to answer the question concerning plans regarding current EU perspective 2014-2020. The vast majority, up to 72%, are interested in further applying for EU funds, 24% were not yet decided (see figure No. 8). Thus, it can be concluded that despite difficulties concerning filling the application to receive EU funding along with the settlement application, the benefits from the grant are higher than the incurred variety of costs.

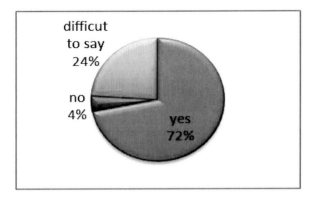

Figure 8: Applying for funding from a current perspective in years 2014-2020 (Own research)

6   Summary and final conclusions

The results of fragmented research conducted by the author on a group of SMEs in Poland allow to make the following conclusions:

1. The most important reason for which companies want to implement ESF projects was to improve the qualifications of employees.
2. Training needs were usually identified by managers or employees themselves who indicated the type of training they would like to participate in.
3. In the surveyed enterprises in most cases the project was directed to all employees.
4. Computer training, foreign language and interpersonal skills dominated in the projects.

5. Effectiveness of training and development were evaluated based on the response and partially through the knowledge level check.

6. One of the results of participation in the project which was most frequently mentioned was improving qualifications of employees.

7. Too complicated application forms caused most difficulties in the process of application for EU grants.

8. Any difficulties during implementation of the project were connected with excessive meticulousness of clerks and delays in payments.

9. Vast majority of enterprises aims to apply again for a grant from the ESF.

It is worthy of note that the issue concerning the use of ESF designated to development of human resources arouses more and more interest. It is presumed to keep growing particularly with respect to a greater sum of financing allocated to Poland by the ESF intended to implementation of activities in the 2014-2020 financial perspective. It is therefore necessary to consider further continuation of theoretical and empirical exploration in this area, which will allow not only to enrich scientific knowledge and rationalize research methodology, but also to formulate useful recommendations for economic practice.

References

Brown, L., Murphy E., Wade V. (2006). Corporate eLearning: Human Resource Development Implications for Large and Small Organizations. *Human Resource Development International*, *3*, 415-427.

Chaston, I. (1997). Small firm performance: assessing the interaction between enterpreneurial style and organizational structure. *European Journal of Marketing*, *31* (11/12), 814-831.

Gibb, A. (1997). Small firms training and competitiveness: building upon the small business as a learning organization, *International Small Business Journal*, *15*(3),13-29.

Grewiński, M. (2001). *Europejski Fundusz Społeczny jako instrument integracja socjalnej Unii Europejskiej*. Warszawa: TWP.

Hill, R., Stewart, J. (1999). Human resource development in small organizations. *Human Resource Development International*, *2*(2), 103-123.

Kirkpatrick, D. L., Kirkpatrick, J. (1994). *Evaluating Training Programs: The Fourth Levels*. San Francisco: Berrett-Koehler Publishers.

Lane, A. D. (1994). Issues in People Management. *People Management in Small and Medium Enterprises*, *8*, London: IPD.

Listwan, T. (1995). *Kształtowanie kadry menedżerskiej firmy*. Wrocław: Wydawnictwo Kadry.

Ministry of Infrastructure and Development. (2016). *Sprawozdanie z wdrażania Programu Operacyjnego Kapitał Ludzki 2007–2013 za I półrocze 2015 roku*. https://www.efs.2007-2013.gov.pl/AnalizyRaportyPodsumowania/poziom/Documents/Sprawozdanie_POKL_I_polrocze_2015.pdf.

Polska Agencja Rozwoju Przedsiębiorczości. (2013). *Bilans Kapitału Ludzkiego w Polsce. Najważniejsze wyniki III edycji badań BKL z 2012 roku.* Warszawa.

Pauli, U. (2014). *Rola szkoleń pracowników w rozwoju małych i średnich przedsiębiorstw*. Kraków: Wydawnictwo Uniwersytetu Ekonomicznego w Krakowie.

Pocztowski, A., Pauli, U. (2013). Profesjonalizacja zarządzania zasobami ludzkimi w małych i średnich przedsiębiorstwach. *Zarządzanie zasobami ludzkimi, 3-4*, 9-22.

Sheehan, M., Pocztowski, A. (2013). Od redakcji. *Zarządzanie zasobami ludzkimi,6*, 7–11.

Storey, D.J. (1994). *Understanding the Small Business Sector*. London: Routledge.

Suchodolski, A. (2010). Rozwój i zarządzanie karierą pracowników. In T. Listwan (Ed.), *Zarządzanie kadrami*. Warszawa: C.H. Beck.

Tracz-Krupa, K. (2014). Human Resource Development within European Social Fund in Poland. *Edukacja Ekonomistów i Menedżerów, 3* (33), 67-82.

Tracz-Krupa K. (2015). Rozwój zasobów ludzkich – przegląd wybranych badań empirycznych w literaturze przedmiotu. *Marketing i Rynek, 5/2015*, 1094-1106.

Trochimiuk, R. (2013). Rozwój zawodowy pracowników w małych i średnich przedsiębiorstwach. *Zarządzanie zasobami ludzkimi, 3-4*, 127-138.

Ustawa o swobodzie działalności gospodarczej z dnia 2 lipca 2004 roku, Dz. U., nr 173, poz. 1807.

Westhead, P., Storey, D.(1997). *Training Provision and the Development of Small and Medium-size Enterprises*. DfEE Publications Research report no 26.

Zarębski, M. (2010). Rola Europejskiego Funduszu Społecznego w rozwoju zasobów ludzkich. *Acta Universitatis Nicoli Copernici*, (397),111-121.

Żukowska, J. (2012). Wpływ szkoleń pracowników na konkurencyjność polskich przedsiębiorstw. In M.A. Weresa (Ed.), *Polska. Raport o konkurencyjności 2012. Edukacja jako czynnik konkurencyjności*. Warszawa: Szkoła Główna Handlowa Oficyna Wydawnicza.

5   GENERATIONAL   COMPARISONS   IN   WORK   VALUES   AND LEADERSHIP MOTIVATION: IS GENERATION Y SPECIAL?

Susanne Rank & Helene Lais

TABLE OF CONTENTS

Abstract

The article explores the work values, traits and leadership motivation of Generation Y (born after 1980) in contrast to preceding generations. The central issues deal with the questions as to what extent Generation Y shows different work values from preceding generations (especially Generation X) and how differently they are motivated to pursue leadership positions in professional work life than the previous Generation X. The results of review concerning Generation Y are not as homogenous as expected but rather even more heterogeneous. Within the review the limitations are discussed as most studies were conducted in Anglo-American regions rather than in Asian regions.

Mail contact: susanne.rank@hs-mainz.de

1   Introduction

Current studies assume that in 2025 around 50-70 % of organizations' workforce around the globe will composed of a generation, which has been the centre of attention for many years, Generation Y (Coleman, 2014; Elance-oDesk, 2015). The term "generation" is defined as a cohort of people who were born in and shaped by a particular span of time (Twenge, 2010). Although each generation naturally consists of heterogeneous and diverse individuals, they are proposed to share a common value system and thoughts distinguishing them from other generations because of shared historical and cultural events. The proposed differences between generations are critically debated as age rather than generational effects on work values within the review of Parry & Urwin (2011). In Anglo-American research (Strauss & Howe, 1991) four working generations are commonly specified in the workforce: *Baby Boomers, Generation X, Generation Y and Generation Z.* The *Veterans*, are already retired and therefore not considered here as there is less impact on HRM concepts in the companies anymore. The first three are explained in the following. The youngest generation, *Generation Z,* is not relevant for this review, because they have only had a few years of working experience at this point in time.

We focus on Generation Y to draw conclusions for HR managers how to deal with these young professionals in companies. However, the preceding Generation X is used as a benchmark to draw meaningful generational comparisons. Different authors use slightly different birth ranges to categorize generations. For example, for Generation Y the lowest year of birth indicated in research is 1978, while the upper limit is as high as 2002 (Tolbize, 2008; DGFP, 2011). Table 1 shows the range of years used for the three generations analysed in this research, with the accompanying ages in the year 2015.

Table 1: Range of years and ages of Baby Boomer, Generation X and Generation Y

	Baby Boomer	Gen X	Gen Y
Birth Ranges	1946 - 1964	1965 - 1979	1980 - 1994
Age in 2016	51 – 70	36 - 51	21 - 36

Source: Tolbize (2008)

However, Generation Y seems to attract a special kind of attention in practitioners' HR papers. The following table 2 provides a brief overview about generational characteristics shared by the popular management literature:

Table 2: Comparison of attitudes and value among three generations

Generation	Characteristics
Baby Boomer	• This generation was marked by dramatic social changes and political turmoil while growing up and have experienced growing consumerism and prosperity in the aftermath of World War II. (Gentry et al., 2011). • Boomers are characterized as being optimistic and seeking self-fulfilment, which could be derived from their notion of a promising future after the war. They are generally described as successful and as workaholics, a term introduced by this generation (Robert Half, 2010).
Generation X	• This generation grew up in economic uncertainty and is often characterized as being risk-tolerant. They have become familiar with technology and are comfortable with diversity, but also consider themselves individualistic and self-reliant (Gentry et al., 2011).
Generation Y	• They are the first generation that grew up in the digital age with dramatic technological advances and possibilities. Generation Y shares many characteristics with their direct predecessor Generation X, while also inhabiting their own distinguishing characteristics as a diverse generation (Tolbize, 2008).

Generation	Characteristics
Generation Y	Because of their upbringing they are comfortable with technology and digitally connected, very confident and ambitious with a desire for freedom, flexible and adaptable to change, value team working and networking, but are also independent, care for social responsibility with a multicultural ease as well as place high value on education and are optimistic (Tolbize, 2008; Hewlett, Sherbing, Sumber, 2009; Twenge et al., 2010)

Whenever an age group or generation is characterized to help HR manager set up appropriate HR concepts to attract Generation Y, at the same time one should be very careful with stereotyping these people because of belonging to a certain generation. However, this stereotyping effect of perceiving Generation Y as a homogenous group could be explained by the social identity group (Tajfel, & Turner, 1979, 1986) as an in- vs. out-group effect. For example, by differentiating the own group (e.g. Generation X) from the other group (Generation Y), the group Y is said to possess special, "strange" features as the perceived out-group, whereas at the same time the own group X is perceived as better than the other group Y (i.e. in-group favouritism)

The consistent generalisations of generational cohorts by popular media rarely match the findings of scientific research. However, an example for a large representative survey of consulting companies revealed generational differences. In the Deloitte's Millennial Survey (2014) nearly 7,800 Millennials from 28 countries across Western Europe, North America, Latin America, BRICS and Asia-Pacific were surveyed about business, government and innovation. The questionnaire focused on the role business plays in society, its objectives and impact. More than half of Generation Y's future leaders might not favour traditionally organized business, prefer to work independently and on their own individual terms. Werle (2012) describes the motivation and willingness of Generation Y to strive for a career in a leadership position as apparently diminishing. From their daily experiences (i.e. face validity perspective) the HR managers confirm that these young talents have completely different expectations than previous generations, e.g. how to get a leader within a company and what kind of development programs should support them including flexible working programs and sabbaticals during this development. However, four generations are working side by side in companies. Generation Y makes up 30 % of the workforce, while Generation X and Baby Boomers make up 52 % and 18 %, respectively (Elance-oDesk, 2014). Many countries are facing an ageing workforce population and an impending shortage of experienced executive managers. The retirement of older generations and the constant incoming of members of Generation Y to the workplace are significant issues for companies. Thus, there are practical implications when it comes to recruitment and management of organization's workforce and future leaders (Twenge et al., 2010, 2012). Is this really true and empirically proven for Generation Y that this generation is special? The academic research shows a different empirical pattern within their studies which are now introduced.

2   Generational comparisons in work values

Generational cohorts are defined as being distinct from each other mainly because of the year of birth. As a consequence, they grew up with similar life experiences, similar values, common historical and social events that are shared by all members of the cohort. These shared features of individuals, born in the same period, influence their social patterns and behaviours in their personal and professional work life. Parry & Urwin (2011) discussed the sociological foundations for the term "generation" as *age-related influences on work values*.[3] This implies that the previous generations impact the following generations by their social bonding in family systems or even more in their specific societies of a local country culture. However, the specific term "generation" is criticised as an artificially divided group in age groups or cohort. Understanding Generation Y helps not only to discover how this generation behaves in the work environment. It can also indicate how they will behave as future leaders in organizations. Therefore, the focus of this review is on Generation Y, their work values and attitudes as predictors for their future commitment in companies in contrast

---

[3] Parry & Urwin (2011, p. 84) provide specific definitions of the terms generation, cohorts, age effects and period effects in their table 1. The term generation is further used a proxy for cohorts.

to the previous Generation X. Concerning these generational differences in work values two major review papers by Twenge (2010) and Parry & Urwin (2011) are discussed in depth. Before summarizing their conclusions methodological limitations should be considered. Some of studies used a cross-sectional design for proofing these generational differences. This is a methodological problem for academic research as the effects are confounded with the other variables like age, tenure, job function or career stage within a company or minority status. From the methodological perspective, a "perfect" academic study should use the time-lag method by studying generational differences over time for specific age groups or different generations. This time-lag method, compared to one-time, cross sectional studies, analyses people at the same age at different time periods. Consequently, any differences must be caused by the generational cohort they belong to rather than by the age they are. A further limitation of generational studies is that most of studies were conducted in the USA, Australia or Europe. Therefore, for future research cultural aspects of different countries should be included as the greatest cultural differences occur between Europe / North America and Asia (Hofstede, 2005, House et al., 2004).

Concerning the work values, Schwartz et al (2012) assume that "values are one important, especially central component of our self and personality, distinct from attitudes, beliefs, norms, and traits". Values are critical motivators of behaviours and attitudes. His values concept was validated across countries and surprisingly found similar value structures.

However, the assessed work value concepts differ from study to study summarized in both reviews of Twenge (2010) and Parry & Urwin (2011) which limited the comparison. In most studies the generations Baby Boomer, X and Y are compared concerning work values. From current HRM practitioners' perspectives, while facing the demographic war of talents, the most interesting focus is on Generation Y in comparison to the previous Generation X. Therefore, the following studies of both reviews (Twenge, 2010; Parry & Urwin, 2011) regarding the last ten years have been selected to draw a comparison of Generation Y vs. X.[4] We include both approaches, i.e. time-lag vs. cross-sectional studies to give HR managers a broad overview.

Busch et al. (2008) showed in an Australian cross-sectional study that Generation Y and X are less interested in unpaid overtime than Baby Boomers. In a cross-sectional study of Cennamo & Gardner (2008) in Australia the Generation Y evaluated the freedom (defined as work life balance) more than Generation X and Baby Boomers. However, no generational differences were identified for extrinsic values, but rather a significant increase in status-related work values from Baby Boomer to Generation X and Y. Further, Generation Y reported a higher likelihood to leave the company than the previous generations. However, no generational differences were found in job satisfaction and organizational commitment. Dries et al (2008) revealed in a cross-sectional study with European workers that Generation Y favours job security more than previous generations.

In a time-lag study Twenge et al. (2010) examines generational differences in work values with data collected over time in three different years (US high school students in 1976, 1991 and 2006) to separate generational differences from age and career differences. In the study of Twenge et al (2010) they differentiate between extrinsic and intrinsic values. Extrinsic work values are tangible rewards - external to an individual and the outcome of work achieved (e.g. income, status or advancement opportunities). Intrinsic values are intangible rewards of work. They focus on the process of work itself rather than the outcome (e.g. opportunity to be creative or learning potential work offers). Some other work values include influence, autonomy, job security, social or leisure rewards (Twenge et al., 2010). In comparison to older generations in the workforce (Baby Boomer and Generation X), Generation Y significantly places *stronger value on leisure time* (Twenge et al., 2010). Furthermore, Generation Y values work that provides *extrinsic rewards* more than previous

---

[4] Due to the dynamic globalization and changes in multiple international enterprise ten years are chosen as a time window for picking out the studies' results.

generations, which actually seems contrary to their value of more leisure time. On the other hand, Generation Y shows a declining importance of intrinsic values. Compared to Baby Boomers at the same age, Generation X and Y rated goals related to extrinsic values (money, image, fame) more important than intrinsic values (self-acceptance, affiliation, community). Finally, social rewards are said to be less important to Generation Y than to the previous two generations, indicating that they feel a lower need to belong to work groups (Twenge et al., 2010).

In a cross-sectional study Ng, Schweitzer and Lyons (2010) investigated the career expectations of Generation Y and explored differences among this cohort related to demographic factors (i.e., gender, race, and years of study) and academic performance. The data base was a national survey of millennial undergraduate university students from across Canada. Generation Y placed the greatest importance on individualistic aspects of a job; they had realistic expectations of their first job and salary but were seeking rapid advancement and the development of new skills, while also ensuring a meaningful and satisfying life outside of work. Ng et al. (2010) stated that: "Millennials' expectations and values significantly vary by gender, visible minority status, GPA, and year of study, but these variables explain only a small proportion of variance." According to Ng et al. (2010), Generation Y puts strong emphasis on a substantial work-life balance and chooses work that does not compromise their private life in an excessive way. They expect good and fair pay and benefits from their work, which might reflect their sense of entitlement and also their self-imposed high personal standards.

Parry & Urwin (2011) discussed in their review the cross-sectional study in US hospitality sector of Chen & Choi (2008). The latter revealed that Generation Y favoured work environment higher than the previous generations. Further, Generation Y was less concerned about personal growth than economic returns. Parry & Urwin (2011) added an interesting aspect to the generational debate about differences in valuing workplace fun. Lamm & Meeks (2009) investigate how generational differences moderate the relationship between workplace fun and individual workplace outcomes in cross-sectional US study. They found that the generation membership moderates the impact of workplace fun on job satisfaction and organizational citizenship behaviour.

Keeping in mind that all reviewed studies were conducted in USA and Europe an Asian study could be added by Kuchinke, Kang, Oh, (2008). They ran an empirical study of Korean mid-level employees in cross-sectional study investigating the effects of different understandings of work and non-work dimensions on job satisfaction, career satisfaction, and organizational commitment. Age differences were found for overall meaning of work. Non-work related dimensions appeared unrelated to work-related outcome variables. The authors concluded that to a limited degree age related differentiation exists in relation to work meaning and separation of work and non-work domains for work-related effects.

As Macky Gardner & Forsyth (2008) state in their article, most of the studies have been conducted in the Anglo-American culture, which show similar cultural values, e.g. concerning individualism (see Hofstede, 2005; House et al., 2005). However, the Asian values show higher collectivism in contrast to Europe and North America. The globalization could impact the younger generation showing similar cultural pattern, e.g. concerning individualism. In contrast to this argument, the popular study of Ashridge Business School (2012) revealed in its international survey with 1789 participants that "national culture has an impact on the way graduates and managers view the world of work, but in a global economy it impacts managers more than graduates." Therefore, more cross-cultural research is necessary to understand similar vs. different generational work values across the European, American vs. Asian work cultures.

In summary, the aesthetic, flexible, fun work place with extrinsic rewards as well as individual development and feedback seems to be preferred by Generation Y. However, the generational differences on work values are rather small and heterogeneous across studies than fundamentally large in contrast to the previous generations. Further, they could be confounded with factors like age or maturity in the business or managerial status or even gender. From an academic perspective time-lag studies only count for empirical evidence; however, for the HR manager of a company even slight differences need to be considered to adapt traditional HR concepts, especially incentives strategies attracting and retaining Generation Y.

3   Generational differences in personality traits and leadership motivation

Moving a step forward to the personality of leaders, their individual traits influence their leadership behaviour (Kaiser & Hogan, 2011). Judge & Hies (2002) tested in their meta-analysis whether there is a relationship between the big five personality dimensions[5] and performance motivation and confirmed their assumption. The most frequent choice of the triple career paths[6] in companies is traditional career progress in the form of a managerial career. Therefore, generational differences in personality traits and motivation could predict a change in traditional career assumptions.

Gentile, Twenge & Campell (2001, 2009) showed in their cross-sectional US study that generations differ on personality traits relevant to work place. Generation Y displayed an increase in positive and negative traits, i.e. higher self-esteem, narcissism, anxiety, and depression; lower need for social approval; more external locus of control[7] and women with more agentic traits.

In the cross-sectional study of Wong et al. (2008) Australian employees filled in the personality questionnaire of SHL, QPQ, and motivation questionnaire to obtain generational differences. Generation Y and X scored higher on the personality traits *achieving* than Baby Boomers whereas no differences on *immersion*, i.e. working more than required. However, the results revealed age effects instead of generational effects.

---

[5] Big five dimensions of personality traits are openness to experience, conscientiousness, extraversion, agreeableness, and neuroticism (Norman, 1963).

[6] The modern career concept in companies consists a triple path approach: manager, project lead and expert.

[7] Internal locus of control (LOC) is a trait (Rotter, 1966, 1975, 1990) that individual tend to attribute outcomes of events to their own control; external locus of control means to attribute outcomes of events to external circumstances.

Sessa et al. (2007) used two large US databases, including managers from four generations in their cross-sectional study. They explored differences occurring among managers of different generations in terms of attributes they value in leaders and their actual behaviour as leaders. The first study demonstrates that "Generation Y prefers a dedicated and creative leader who cares about them personally (encouraging, listens well, supportive). Big-picture orientation does not appear in their top rankings. Although they value trustworthiness, they do not place it as high as other groups. Higher values in dedication, focus, and optimism, along with lower values in credibility and farsightedness, differentiate Generation Y from other generations". In the second study managers of different generations report behaving differently. The generational differences in both studies are not as fundamental. The authors stated that "organizations do need to pay attention to these differences: Leaders in the younger generations bring an energizing presence; they are focused on attaining short-term results; and they are more self-focused ". However, Parry & Urwin (2011) argued that the differences are be linked even more with the maturational stage in a company than impacted by a generational cohort effect.

Dries et al. (2008) explored generational differences in career types in a Belgian sample in a cross-sectional research design. A vignette task should be completed by rating the career success of 32 fictitious people. Each vignette contained a specific combination of five career attributes (functional level, salary, number of promotions, promotion speed, and satisfaction). It is the first study which examines career success evaluation by an experimental design using the means of vignettes. The majority of participants favoured "traditional" careers. Overall, satisfaction appeared to be the overriding criterion used to evaluate other people's career success. No significant differences were found between generations. Generation Y (and the silent generation) scored significantly higher organizational security than the other generations.

D' Amato and Herzfeldt (2008) tested the relationships of learning, organizational commitment and talent retention across generations by asking European managers. Generation X shows stronger learning orientation and lower organizational commitment than Baby Boomers. For Generation X learning orientation predicted the intention to remain in the same organization. Organizational commitment mediated this relationship. However, Generation Y was not included.

In sum, few studies explored generational differences on personality traits, leadership motivation and career expectations. The Generation Y showed higher self-esteem, narcissism, more external locus of control in to contrast to higher anxiety, and depression as well as a lower need for social approval compared to previous generations. Generation Y favoured more individualistic, creative leaders. Only one study investigated the leadership motivation of Generation Y (Wong et al, 2008): Their achievement motivation was high but similar to Generation X.

Further, these studies are conducted in USA and Europe. Focusing on cross-cultural perspective, there is evidence that Europeans place higher value on the personality trait locus of control than Asian people (LOC, i.e. a pro-active attitude to make things happen). The high individualism of the Anglo-American culture is found to correlate strongly with internal LOC (Spector et al., 2001). Parry & Urwin (2011) assume that cultural effects might be stronger than generational effects on work values. For future research the scope of research should be extended to different regions, e.g. Asia.

Moreover, leadership research (see van Iddekinge et al., 2009) proposes a *multistage model* including *distal, semi-distal and proximal drivers* for leadership performance. Examples for *distal drivers* are cognitive ability or personality trait as already discussed. For *semi-distal influencer leadership motivation* or experience are proposed. Finally, good examples for *proximal antecedents* are knowledge, skill, and abilities.

Due to slightly different work values and personality traits of Generation Y wwe suggest that Generation Y shows a different pattern of leadership motivation (as semi-distal influencer) for filling in a leadership position than previous generations: Generation Y critically calculates what is in it for me instead of showing obligation as do previous generations. This hypothesis was tested in a preliminary master thesis study by Lais (2015) applying the motivational leadership concept of Felfe & Gatzka

Affective	Non-Calculative	Social-Normative
"... because I enjoy doing it"	"... because I don't care if there will be any benefits for me"	"... because it is expected from me"

Figure 1: Facets of Leadership Motive by Felfe & Gratzka (2012)

(2012) who build on Chan and Drasgow's research. They define *Motivation to Lead* (MtL) as the individual preference to aspire to leadership responsibilities (Elprana & Hernandez Bari, 2014)[8]. MTL is as a strong predictor for leadership potential, participation in leadership training, leader emergence and leadership performance (Stiehl, Felfe, Elprana & Gatzka, 2016). MTL splits into three different facets shown in figure 1: *Affective facet* (emphasizes positive and internal emotional feelings towards leadership tasks), *non-calculative facet* (doesn't look for any advantages or disadvantages coming from leading) and *social-normative facet* (stirred by a feeling of duty and expectations by others (Felfe & Gratzka, 2012).If all motives are congruent, a strong intrinsic motivation develops, while a deviation will lead to barriers and inner conflicts concerning leadership responsibility (Felfe & Gatzka, 2012). This MTL concept was chosen as we assume it is sensitive to discover the special generational differences because the Generation Y calculates the individual benefit of becoming a leader.

In the preliminary study conducted by Lais (2015) as part of her master's thesis research, a sample of German Generation Y (students) and Generation X (managers) participated. To discover differences in leadership motivation besides the three basic motive of McClelland et al. (1982, power, achievement and affiliation) MTL and

---

[8] In this research, the terms "Motivation to Lead" and "leadership motivation" will be used interchangeably, both referring to a specific motivation to assume and take on leadership responsibilities. Another definition of leadership motivation is the individual impulse to lead and the willingness to undertake managerial responsibility (Simonsen, 2013).

motivational barriers (Felfe et al. 2012) are included in the questionnaire. We assume that the students of Generation Y possess a lower affective MTL than previous generations as they calculate more what they hope to gain (because of high self-esteem and narcissism). Similarly, they also possess a lower normative MTL than preceding generations as they are more self-focused than being totally committed to the company. They would only take on leadership positions out of their own conviction, as they believe it would benefit their own personal development. Therefore, the students of Generation Y possess a higher calculative MTL than managers of Generation X. We argue that Generation Y takes on leadership roles if there are extrinsic values given. Higher leadership avoidance of students of Generation Y is expected compared to the managers of Generation X. The study only is preliminary to explore the proposed hypotheses; however, a co-founding effect of age/generation and managerial status are included; but they are controlled. No differences were found regarding the three basic motives (power, achievement and affiliation) of Mc Cleeland et al. (1982). However, MTL results show a significant difference for the affective and calculative facet of MTL between students of Generation Y vs. the managers of Generation X. The students of Generation Y had a significantly lower score of affective MTL than managers of Generation X. Affective MTL is probably the most important motive to have when assuming a leadership position as it is most effective predictor of leadership emergence (Elprana et al., 2016). However, the students of Generation Y displayed higher values for calculative facets of MTL than the managers of Generation X. No significant differences for normative facets occurred. The students of Generation Y show higher leadership avoidance than the manager of Generation X. One reason for the low score could be that they still have some concerns about what exactly their road to a leadership position as they are young professionals. In general, confounding effects of age /maturity as well as of gender (Elprana et al, 2016) need to be tested in a follow up study.

For our future research, we suggest to extend this study design by including work values or career preferences to understand the driver for the leadership motivation of the different age groups/generations. Further, the cross-cultural perspective with different regions should be integrated as discussed earlier. For the HR manager different motivational pattern are important to be considered for customizing the HR concepts.

4   Conclusion

Within companies the motivational differences for leadership should be carefully considered for retention programs of future employees and leaders. Especially for international companies the cross-cultural view on work values and leadership motivation is worth considering in order to know how to recruit, develop and retain future leaders of Generation Y. The challenge for HR managers might be to customize the employer branding programs, talent management and leadership development as well as the flexible, funny workplace concepts to generational and cultural demands.

For outlook on future research an additional aspect should be taken in account: The Corporate Social Responsibility or Corporate Social Performance (CSR or CSP, used similar, i.e. stakeholder approach focusing on economic and duty-aligned, social demands) which impacts employer branding program of (international) companies. Greeing and Turban (2000) point out in their research with American college students of Generation Y that CSP is important factor for these highly skilled employees applying more for a new job in a company with CSP than without CSP. However, this effect might be true for North America and Europe in contrast to Asia. Ho, Wang, Vitell (2011) show in an international study that four dimensions of Hofstede are related to CSP. Peng et al. (2010) reveal a different pattern but cultural dimensions and CSP are also related. Further, as a part of the overall CSP strategy of company the Workplace CSP describes an employee-friendly work place impacting the entire HR process map; i.e. recruitment, workforce diversity, pay and working conditions, health and safety and recognition of trade unions (European Commision, 2009). Bustamente & Brenninger (2013) showed for German students that this Workplace CSP is requirement ("must have") for choosing a future workplace. Therefore, the research on work values and leadership motivation might be extended by the Workplace CSP to evaluate and customize the entire HR process map concerning the expectation of the younger Generation Y. Moreover, future studies should include a cross-cultural focus including different regions like USA, Europe and Asia. However, strong cultural differences are to be expected to moderate the minor generational pattern on work values and leadership motivation.

References

Ashridge Business School (2012). Culture schock: Generation Y and their managers around the world. www.ashridge.org.uk. 11/21/16.

Busch, P, Venkitachalam, K. & Richards, D. (2008) Generational Differences in Soft Knowledge Situations: Status, Need for Recognition, Workplace Commitment and Idealism. *Knowledge and Process Management*, 15(1), 45–58.

Bustamante, S. & Brenninger, K. (2013). CSR and its Potential Role in Employer Branding: An Analysis of Preferences of German Graduates. ISIS Report University of Graz, 6, 31-54.

Cennamo, L. & Gardner, D. (2008). Generational differences in work values, outcomes and person-organisation values fit. *Journal of Managerial Psychology*, 23(8), 891 – 906.

Chan, K. and Drasgow, F. (2001). Toward a Theory of Individual Differences and Leadership: Understanding the Motivation to Lead. *Journal of Applied Psychology*, 86(3), 481-498.

Chen, P. and Choi, Y. (2008). Generational differences in work values: a study of hospital management. *International Journal of Contemporary Hospitality Management*, 20, 595–615.

Constantine, G. (2010). Tapping Into Generation Y: Nine Ways Community Financial Institutions Can Use Technology to Capture Young Customers http://www.firstdata.com/downloads/thought-leadership/geny_wp.pdf 11/22/16.

Coleman, M. (2014). In Times of Transition, Employee Recognition is More Important Than Ever. http://www.myemployees.com/blog/in-times-of-transition-employee-recognition-is-more-important-than-ever. 11/22/16.

D'Amato, A. Herzfeldt, R. (2008). Learning orientation, organizational commitment and talent retention across generations: A study of European managers. *Journal of Managerial Psychology*, 23(8), 929 – 953

Deloitte (2014). Big demands and high expectations. The Deloitte Millenial Survey. http://www2.deloitte.com/al/en/pages/about-deloitte/articles/2014-millennial-survey-positive-impact.html. 10/28/16.

Dries, N., Pepermans, R.& De Kerpel, E. (2008) Exploring four generations' beliefs about career: Is "satisfied" the new "successful"? *Journal of Managerial Psychology*, 23(8), 907 – 928.

DGFP e.V., (2011). Zwischen Anspruch und Wirklichkeit: Generation Y finden, fördern und binden. Deutsche Gesellschaft für Personalführung e.V. (Ed.). Praxis Paper 9/2011.

Elance-oDesk and MillennialBranding (Ed.) (2015). Generation Y: Herausforderungen und Chance. http://www.crowdsourcingblog.de/wp-content/uploads/2015/01/Elance-oDesk_GenerationY_Studienergebnisse.pdf. 11/22/16.

Elprana, G., Felfe, J., Stiehl S. & Gatzka, M. (2016). Exploring the sex-difference in affective Motivation to Lead. Furthering the understanding of women's underrepresentation in leadership positions. *Journal of Personnel Psychology*. 14(3), 142-152.

Elprana, G. & Hernandez Bark, A. S. (2014). Frauen in Führungspositionen – Aktuelle Förderansätze. In J. Felfe (Ed.). Aktuelle Entwicklungen in der Führungsforschung. Göttingen: Hogrefe Verlag.

European Commission. (2009). European Competitiveness Report 2008: Communication from the Commission COM (2008) 774 final. Luxemburg: Office for Official Publications of the European Communities.

Felfe, J. & Gatzka, M. (2012). Führungsmotivation. In: W. Sarges (Ed.). Managementdiagnostik. Göttingen: Hogrefe Verlag.

Gentile, B., Twenge, J. M., & Campbell, W. K. (2010). Birth cohort differences in self-esteem, 1988–2008: A cross-temporal meta-analysis. *Review of General Psychology*, 14, 261–268.

Gentry, W.A. et al. (2011). A Comparison of Generational Differences in Endorsement of Leadership Practices with Actual Leadership Skill Level. Consulting Psychology Journal: Practice and Research, 63(1), 39-49.

Greening, D. W., & Turban, D. B. 2000. Corporate social performance as a competitive advantage in attracting a quality workforce. *Business and Society*, 39(3), 254-303.

Hewlett, S.A., Sherbin, L. and Sumberg, K., (2009). How Gen Y & Boomers will reshape your agenda. *Harvard Business Review*, July-August, 1-8.

Ho, F., Wang, H., & Vitell, S. (2011). A Global Analysis of Corporate Social Performance: The Effects of Cultural and Geographic Environments. *Journal of Business Ethics*, 107(4), 423-433.

Hofstede, G. (2005). Cultures Consequences. Sage Publications.

House, R.J, Hanges, P.J., Javidan, M., Dorfman, P. W. & Gupta, V. (2004). Culture, Leadership and Organizations. Sage Publications.

Kuchinke, K.P., Kang, HS. & Oh, SY. (2008). The influence of work values on job and career satisfaction, and organizational commitment among Korean professional level employees. *Asia Pacific Educ. Review*, 9(4), 552–564.

Kaiser, R. B. & Hogan, J. (2011). Personality, leader behavior and overdoing it. Consulting Psychology Journal: Practice and Research, 63, 219 – 242.

Judge, T. A. & Hies, R. (2002). Relationship of personality to performance motivation: A meta-analytic review. Journal of Applied Psychology, 87, 797–807.

Lais, H. (2015). The Potential of Generation Y as Future Leaders. Unpublished master thesis at the University of Applied Sciences of Mainz.

Macky, K., Gardner, D. Forsyth, S. (2008) Generational differences at work: introduction and overview, *Journal of Managerial Psychology*, 23(8), 857 – 861.

McClelland, D.C. & Boyatzis, R. E. (1982). Leadership motive pattern and long-term success in management. *Journal of Applied Psychology*, 67(6), 737-743.

Ng, E., Schweitzer, L. and Lyons, S.T. (2010). New Generation, Great Expectations: A Field Study of the Millennial Generation. *Journal of Business Psychology*, 25, 281–292.

Norman, W. T. (1963). Toward an adequate taxonomy of personality attributes: Replicated factor structure in peer nomination personality ratings. *Journal of Abnormal Psychology*, 66, 574–583.

Parry E. & Urwin P. (2010). Generational differences in work values: A review of theory and evidence, *International Journal of Management Reviews*, 13, 79–96.

Peng, Y., Dashdeleg, A., & Chih, H. (2012). Does National Culture Influence Firm's CSR Engagement: A Cross Country Study. International Proceedings of Economics Development & Research, 58, 40-44.

Robert Half (2010). What the different generations want and how they want it. http://www.roberthalf.de/EMEA/Germany/Assets/eDMs/Robert_Half_Viele_Generationen_ein_Team.pdf. 11/22/16.

Rotter, J. B. (1966). Generalized expectancies for internal versus external control of reinforcement. *Psychological Monographs: General & Applied*, 80(1), 1–28.

Rotter, J.B. (1990). Internal versus external control of reinforcement: A case history of a variable. *American Psychologist. 45(4), 489–93.*

Schwartz, S. H., Cieciuch, J., Vecchione, M., Davidov, E., Fischer, R., Beierlein, C., Ramos, A., Verkasalo, M., Lönnqvist, J.-E., Demirutku, K., Dirilen-Gumus, O., & Konty, M. (2012). Refining the theory of basic individual values. *Journal of Personality and Social*, 103(4), 663-88.

Sessa, V. Kabarcoff, R., Deal, J. & Brown, H. (2007) Generational Differences in Leader

Values and Leadership Behaviors. *The Psychologist Manager Journal*, 10(1), 47–74.

Simonsen, B. (2013). Selbstverwirklichung wichtiger als Chef-Sein? Sinn und Selbstbestimmung sind die Boni der Zukunft! http://simonsen-management.de/selbstverwirklichung-der-generation-y-erfordert-neues-fuehrungsverstaendnis/. 11/22/16.

Spector, P E, Cooper, C.L., Sanchez, J.I., O'Driscoll, M., Sparks, K., Bernin, P., Büssing, A. Dewe, P., Hart, P. Lu, L. Miller, K., Flavio, L. De Moraes, R., Ostrognay, G.M, Pagon, M. Pitariu, H., Poelmans, S., Radhakrishnan, P. Russinova, V., Salamatov, V., Salgado, J., Shima, S., Siu, L.O, Benjamin, J., Teichmann, M.S., Theorell, T., Vlerick, P., Westman, M., Widerszal Bazyl, M., Wong, P., Yu, S. (2001). Do national levels of individualism and internal locus of control relate to well-being: an ecological level international study. *Journal of Organizational Behavior*, 22, 815-811.

Strauss, W. and Howe, N. (1991). Generations: The History of America's Future, 1584–2069. New York: William Morrow.

Stiehl, S., Felfe, J., Elprana, G., & Gatzka, M. (2016). The role of motivation to lead for leadership training effectiveness. *International Journal of Training and Development*, 19(2), 1360-3736.

Stiehl, S., Gatzka, M., Elprana, G. & Felfe, J. (2015). Personality and Leadership Intention: The Mediating Role of Motivation to Lead for Career Aspirations. *Zeitschrift für Arbeits- und Organisationspsychologie, 59,* 188-205.

Tajfel, H., & Turner, J. C. (1979, 1986). The social identity theory of intergroup behavior. In Austin, W.G.; Worchel, S. (Eds.) Psychology of Intergroup Relations. Chicago: Nelson-Hall.

Tolbize, A. (2008) Generational differences in the workplace. Research and Training Center on Community Living. University of Minnesota. http://rtc.umn.edu/docs/2_18_Gen_diff_workplace.pdf.11/22/16.

Twenge, J. M. (2010). A review of the empirical evidence on generational differences in work attitudes. *Journal of Business Psychology,* 25, 201 210.

Twenge, J. M., Campbell, S.M., Hoffman, B.J. and Lance, C.E. (2010). Generational Differences in Work Values: Leisure and Extrinsic Values Increasing, Social and Intrinsic Values Decreasing. *Journal of Management,* 36, 1117-1141.

Twenge, J.M., Campbell, S.M., Freemann, E. C. (2012) Generational Differences in Young Adults' Life Goals, Concern for Others, and Civic Orientation, 1966–2009. *Journal of Personality and Social Psychology*, 102(5), 1045–1062.

Van Iddekinge, C., Ferris, G., & Heffner, T. (2009). Test of a multistage model of distal and proximal antecedents of leader performance. *Personnel Psychology*, 62, 463-495.

Wong M., Gardiner E., Lang,W. & Coulon, L. (2008). "Generational differences in personality and motivation: Do they exist and what are the implications for the workplace?", *Journal of Managerial Psychology*, 23(8), 878–890.

Werle,   K.   (2012).   Manager   von   morgen.   Geld   oder   Titel   ziehen   kaum. http://www.spiegel.de/karriere/berufsstart/berufseinstieg-wie-firmen-die-manager-von-morgen-sehen-a-869420.html. 11/22/16.

PART II

IHRM PROCESS:

IMPACT AND PRODUCTIVITY

6 INCREASING COMPANIES' PRODUCTIVITY: THE ROLE OF HUMAN RESOURCES

Ulrich Schüle & Ching Yee Au

TABLE OF CONTENTS

Abstract

This paper provides an overview of empirical studies on the role human resources play in productivity enhancement. The purpose is to show how variations in concepts and definitions used in empirical work still make it impossible to develop unambiguous guidelines for companies.

We first discuss the economic importance and possible definitions of productivity, then examine selected HR-related determinants of productivity. We briefly refer to the determinant's relevance, before we analyze empirical studies conducted in Europe, Asia, and the Americas. We then conclude with some suggestions for further research.

Mail contact: ulrich.schuele@hs-mainz.de

1   The Economic Importance of Productivity

Countries' as well as companies' competitiveness depends on productivity as increases in productivity result in decreasing costs per unit and allow for growing income of capital owners and employees. Therefore, productivity enhancement is at the core of long-term macroeconomic growth policies and company strategies.

Productivity improvement is closely related to technical innovation and progress. Whereas in the early years of macroeconomic growth theories (Solow), technical progress either was seen as exogenous variable ("manna from heaven"), or being "embodied" in machinery and equipment (Jorgenson), more modern theories (Romer) explain technology as knowledge creation, mainly as the result of education and research and development (R&D) activities in the public as well as in the private sector: "Because human capital is, by definition, embodied skills and knowledge, and because advances in technical knowledge drive economic growth, it follows that human capital accumulation and economic growth are intimately related" (Topel, 1999, p. 2944). Knowledge creation is not possible without human resources. As a result, macroeconomic research has focused increasingly on the role human resources play for productivity enhancement.

Studies at the microeconomic level laid emphasis on productivity enhancing HRM tools. Besides more obvious productivity-related variables such as payment structures and recruitment policies, researchers identified training, employee turnover, job satisfaction, and employee participation as labor-related determinants of productivity.

Even though many projects analyzed the impact of these determinants on production outcome, a commonly shared, empirically grounded theory still does not exist.

2   Definitions of Productivity

Productivity is generally defined as the relation between output quantity and input quantity. Partial productivities relate the output quantity to the input quantity of one production factor. Thus:

$$Labor\ productivity\quad=\quad\frac{output\ quantity}{quantity\ of\ labour\ input}$$

$$Capital\ productivity\quad=\quad\frac{output\ quantity}{quantity\ of\ capital\ input}$$

Output quantity can be measured as units of products or services produced – which at the macroeconomic level corresponds to GDP[real]. Labor input is typically measured as employee hours worked – at the micro as well as macroeconomic level. The quantity of capital input is typically measured by the value of physical capital (fixed assets); if applicable, microeconomic studies may measure it as the number of machine hours worked.

The problem of partial productivities is that they are inversely related to each other. Factor substitution automatically increases one of the productivities and simultaneously reduces the other. So, if at a given level of output labor is replaced with machines, labor productivity increases while capital productivity decreases. The use of Total Factor Productivity (TFP) avoids this problem.

$$TFP\quad=\quad\frac{output\ quantity}{input\ quantity*\ \lambda+capital\ input*(1-\lambda)}$$

TFP divides the output quantity by both production factors, each of them multiplied with the relative share of the production factor to overall input costs. So, an alteration in TFP reflects all changes in productivity not caused by factor substitution.

A country's as well as a company's growth may be caused by an increase of the input factors labor and capital (extensive growth) or by TFP increases (intensive growth). As neoclassical theories showed, TFP explains the largest part of economies' long-term growth.

In microeconomic studies – thus, in the studies presented below – the measurement of productivity often deviates from these definitions. Especially when related to non-tangible outputs, varying performance measures, including supervisors' subjective evaluation, are used; sometimes, even financial ratios are applied. For example, the quantity of labor input may be replaced with labor cost.

3   Selected Determinants

HRM-related determinants of productivity are many-fold. For a long time, and still relevant in the framework of the principal-agent-theory, payment structures have been seen as crucial for enhancing employees' performance. Bonus systems first introduced in sales-related functions and at the executive level, are nowadays widely applied. In many OECD countries, even for non-executive employees in public administration the traditional service-incremental payment schemes were supplemented with bonus schemes.

Performance determinants may be divided into external (sociological, technological, economic, political) and organizational factors, with the latter being composed of organizational (structure, system, size, history) and people factors (Hansen and Wernerfelt, 1989). In the context of our research, we focus on people factors, using training, employee turnover, job satisfaction, and employee participation as examples.

4   Training

Relevance

It seems to be obvious that productivity depends on employee qualification. Under-qualified workers make more mistakes; they need more time and effort than qualified workers, thus creating lost time, material, and customers. New technologies applied in the work process – in manufacturing as well as in the office environment – require employees to be re-trained. In particular, employees working in a manufacturing or office environment drive by information technologies (IT) need to cope with changes in software and functionalities. Partly, this change is rather gradual and requires not more than some on-the-job-training; partly more extensive training measures may be needed.

Empirical Results

Most of the studies point out that training can increase productivity. According to the meta study of Bartel (2000), three types of studies can be identified. The first type consisting of "large samples of firm-level or establishment-level data collected through mail or phone interviews... was found to provide little guidance" (p. 522), because they rarely relied on objective data and "production processes may not have ben modelled properly" (p. 522). The second largest category consists of econometric studies applied to one or two companies. The third type are case studies. The 16 case studies she scrutinized all suffered from methodological flaws, such as using supervisors' subjective evaluation of trainees' performance levels, self-reports from trainees about the training gains (p. 519). One major problem, however, is that Bartel focuses more on the employer's return than on productivity increases.

In a more recent meta-study, Tharenou et al. (2007) reviewed 67 studies "that have investigated the relationship between training and human resource, performance, and financial outcomes" (p. 251). Their results suggest that "training is positively related to human resource outcomes and organizational performance but is only very weakly related to financial outcomes" (p. 251). Moreover, they suspect that mediators, such as already existing human capital and employee attitudes, may have an impact on the training's effectiveness.

Studies in Europe support the hypothesis of a positive impact of training on productivity. Sala and Silva (2013) used OECD and Eurostat data on 25 European countries and related training hours to labor productivity. Conti (2005) as well as Colombo and Stanca (2014) used panel data of Italian firms. However, the data used in the two latter studies did not allow for separating more formal (even college) education from vocational in-company training. So, the studies may have included productivity increases caused by recruiting high-skilled employees rather than by training.

Apart from general effects of training on productivity, the different forms of training are important. Firstly, the question whether the training is provided on-the-job or off-the-job may influence its productivity increasing effect (Sepulveda 2010; Hara, 2014). Whereas some studies indicate that on-the-job-training increases worker productivity (for example Ariga et al., 2010), others are more sceptical (Zwick, 2005) or relate the result to further conditions (Maliranta and Asplund ,2007).

Secondly, the impacts may differ depending on whether the training focuses on company-specific skills, industry-specific skills or skills which can be used in any company (Kim and Ployhart, 2014). In the German context where industry-wide vocational training certifications are of high importance, the difference between formal external training and non-formalized versions needs to be taken in account (Zwick, 2005). Thirdly, the job position of the trainees and their previous work experience may have a significant influence on the productivity effects of training.

Despite of the many studies, there is no theoretical model providing companies with guidance. As pointed out in the meta studies of Bartel (2000) and Tharenou (2007), large samples of firm-level data collected through questionnaires and interviews rarely measure productivity increases but use subjective supervisors' opinions, econometric studies often measure training too vaguely, and case studies often use supervisors' subjective evaluation of trainees' performance or employees' self-judgment. In addition, it remains unclear how mediators and moderators, such as work attitude, the individual level of human capital, job satisfaction, and wage-related aspects of training, interfere with the studies' results.

5   Employee Turnover

Relevance

There seems to be a wide-spread consensus that employee turnover has an effect on companies' productivity. However, whether this effect is positive or negative is highly controversial.

On the one hand, HRM text books and consultants point out that turnover is costly and HRM should develop "strategies for employee retaining and minimizing turnover" (Yazinski, 2009, p.1). The reason is that employees, who leave the company, take a large part of their knowledge with them – leaving a gap that has to be filled within a time-consuming training process. The more the job requires company-specific knowledge, the higher are the productivity losses and, hence costs for refilling the gap.

On the other hand, the tenured employment conditions in the public sector have been seen as a reason for inefficiencies and low productivity. Therefore, one major objective of public sector reforms in Europe has been "making public sector organizations more flexible, responsive and performance-oriented … driven by the desire for more efficiency, productivity and competitiveness" (Bossaert, 2005, p. 4).

Other theoretical patterns state that "the negative effects of voluntary turnover on performance are attenuated as the rate increases …, and that the turnover-performance relationship is contingent on an organization's human resource investments and inducements" (Shaw et al., 2005, p. 50).

Empirical Results

Most of the research on labor turnover focuses on voluntary turnover – based on the belief and some empirical evidence that high quit rates are costly. "As part of the process of developing and implementing strategies to maintain and increase competitiveness, organizations face the challenge of retaining their best employees." (Ramlall, 2003, p. 64). The focus, therefore, seems to lie on the determinants of the quit decision (Holtom et. al., 2008).

Turnover costs are estimated as being as high as half the employees' yearly salary. These costs comprise the recruiting and hiring cost as well as the costs for training of the newly hired employee. The higher the employees are located in the hierarchy, the more specialized they are, and the more tacit their knowledge is, the more costly are high rates of labor turnover. Mainly U.S. based research stresses the negative impact of voluntary turnover on productive. Among others, examples studies made in the manufacturing sector (Arthur, 1994), financial services (McElroy et al., 2001), and the restaurant industry (Kacmar et al., 2006).

More recent research supports the "attenuation" and "contingency" hypotheses. For example, Shaw et. al. (2005a) point out that the negative impact of "network disruptions" (caused by voluntary quits) was more apparent when overall turnover was low. Siebert and Zubanov (2009) analyzed the relationship between sales assistant turnover and labor productivity in 325 stores of a large U.K. clothing retailer: "We find that the turnover-productivity relationship is contingent on type of work system. For a large group of part-timers, managed under a "secondary" work system, the relationship clearly has an inverted U-shape, but for the smaller group of full-timers, managed under a "commitment" system, the relationship is the conventional negative one." Hancock et el. (2013) reveal that the relation between turnover and organizational performance depends on the measurement of performance. The negative impact of turnover on productivity is stronger, if performance is measured in terms of customer service or quality and safety metrics.

However, employee turnover might also be used for acquiring knowledge. New entrants are often formally more highly qualified than incumbent employees, often younger, highly motivated and willing to sacrifice private life for career opportunities. If, simultaneously, the knowledge of leaving workers can be still used by the worker's former employer, overall mobility results in net inflows of knowledge (Cooper, 2001). Then, a certain level of turnover might be beneficial to the company. Using data from the Danish employer-employee register covering the period 1995–2005, Parrotta and Pozzolli (2012), for example, estimate that hiring "knowledge carriers" increases productivity by 1 to 2 per cent. In particular, R&D driven companies are in continuous need of innovation; for them, a continuous inflow of new ideas and people "thinking against the organizational mainstream" may help keeping the productivity level high. Müller and Peters (2010) reveal that this effect is higher for product innovation than process innovation. Similar scenarios are likely in sectors with a high need for creativity.

Moreover, the impacts of employee turnover on productivity may differ depending on the reasons for turnover. If turnover is caused by dismissals, the impact on productivity should be positive. In contrast, when employees leave at their own request, the impact rather tends to be negative. In case of mass dismissals – when the company must "downsize" – the results cannot be predicted. As companies tend to dismiss the less productive workers, employees might increase their work commitment. On the other hand, such a situation negatively affects the overall work atmosphere, so that the individual incentive to work harder may be over-compensated. Research on employment protection indicates that "stringent employment protection reduces job creation as well as job destruction and weakens firms' ability to exploit new technologies and markets" (Scarpetta, 2014, p.1)

In summary, there is no theoretical model with unambiguous results. Besides the problem of measuring productivity objectively, one possible reason for varying results may be that both variables – productivity and labor turnover – depend on the company's sales performance. Poor sales figures decrease productivity, lower employees' expectations and increase their willingness to quit. Poor sales figures during a recession may lead to productivity-decreasing "labor hoarding" – most probably more in Europe and Japan than in the United States.

6   Job Satisfaction

Relevance

The relation between job satisfaction and productivity has drawn a lot of attention during the last half century. Even though theoretical models range from the idea that job satisfaction increases productivity to the hypothesis that there is no such relation (Judge et al., 2001), there seems to be a market for HRM tools targeting job satisfaction. The Internet is full of advertisement offering companies three/five/seven/ten "ways to boost job satisfaction and productivity".

Empirical Results

In their "meta-analytic review" of 312 samples containing 254 studies, Judge et al. (2001) came to the conclusion that "the correlation between job satisfaction and job performance is moderate in magnitude ... and distinguishable from zero" (p. 385).

They propose a new model in which moderators (for example job characteristics) and mediators (for example behavioral intentions) play a crucial role for the relation between job satisfaction and job performance.

The definition of job satisfaction differs between the studies. In many cases, job satisfaction is simply described as how people feel about their jobs and different aspects of their jobs. It is the extent to which people like (satisfaction) or dislike (dissatisfaction) their jobs. Spector's "Job Satisfaction Survey" is a questionnaire using Likert scales for covering nine dimensions with four questions each (Spector 1985, 1997, 2016).

An alternative approach is based on the assumption that satisfaction depends on expectations – similar to modern concepts of measuring consumer satisfaction (for example the SERVQUAL tool). Thus, workers are satisfied when the "work-role output" – such as wages, status – is higher than the "work-role input" – such as working time and effort (Sousa-Poza and Sousa-Poza, 2000).

EUROFOUND (2007), based on Rose (2001), points out that even the expression "job" is used ambiguously. It may relate to the work contents and tasks to be fulfilled, but simultaneously the "post occupied by the person performing those tasks" (p. 4).

Moreover, problems of measuring need to be addressed.

Appelbaum et al. (2005), for example, studied a rod mill which suffered from chronically low productivity. The authors conducted a survey to measure employee satisfaction and to determine the correlation between employee satisfaction and productivity. The study focused on low-skilled workers and found a correlation between average job satisfaction, low motivation and the resulting low productivity. The methodology applied was based on a standard survey developed by Clear Picture, a Canadian Software company offering – amongst others – online portals for "Employee Listening and Involvement". The measurement was based on the "employee value index" which may not only measure employees' job satisfaction, but also supervisors' performance. The assessment of productivity was measured as operational efficiency, "defined as the ratio of good production to total potential production" (Appelbaum et. al., 2005, p. 2). The figure was clearly below industry average.

In the study of Westlund and Loethgren (2001), employee satisfaction was one aspect measured with twelve items, for example related to tasks, knowledge, autonomy, appreciation. A "Weighted Productivity Indicator" was used to measure the service outcome of pharmacies. The findings supported a positive impact of job satisfaction with productivity.

Halkos and Bousinakis (2010) used a random sample of 425 employees in the private and public sector. The survey measured different aspects of stress and employee satisfaction, such as number of work hours, good relations between management and employees, good function of the group and work related to employees' area of education. The data were collected in form of personal interviews, Likert-scale answers were used mainly. Factor analysis helped to identify moderators for the relation between stress, satisfaction, and productivity. Identified factors were then set into a regression with the dependent, dichotomous variable "effect on productivity". Productivity, defined as output/input relation, was not measured, however.

A survey conducted in Taiwan by Wu et al. (2013) focused on relationship marketing and covered job satisfaction as one of the variables. As in the other studies, productivity was measured in form of subjective assessment by management. The results suggest that job satisfaction has a positive impact on organizational performance. Also Chen et al. (2004) measured the influence of job satisfaction on productivity within a broader context. R&D personnel working in a science-based industrial park were asked about their attitudes towards professional development programs and job satisfaction. Productivity was measured in output categories like patents registered, papers published, and received prizes and awards.

Whereas the former papers tried to find evidence for job satisfaction positively influencing productivity, Christen et al. (2006), based on the principle-agency theory, tried to find empirical evidence for the hypothesis that job performance has a positive impact on job satisfaction. Their model assumes that besides fixed payment and profit sharing various job characteristics and problems with role perceptions determine workers' effort which – in combination with their work ability – determines job performance and, eventually, organizational performance. Based on the results of the study the importance of performance pay was stressed.

Criticism of questionnaire-based studies focus on two issues: Firstly, they typically rely on evaluations made by supervisors about their employees' performance. Secondly, job satisfaction is not only influenced by endogenous variables but also by factors from outside the company. In a Finnish study, Böckerman and Ilmakunnas (2010), therefore, use the concepts of labor productivity, defined as valued added per hours worked, and total factor productivity in the manufacturing sector. In models which include the private service sector, they use turnover (sales) per employee as performance measure. As measure for job satisfaction, they use however a proxy – workers' satisfaction with their housing conditions because they "expect that there exists a positive correlation between job satisfaction and satisfaction with housing conditions, based on the psychology literature" (p. 7). Their results are rather insignificant.

In summary, a coherent, empirically tested theory giving HR policies a clear guidance, still does not exist. One of the reasons for the ambiguous picture empirical studies show is the high variation of definitions and indicators used. Measurements of job satisfaction as well as productivity vary significantly.

7   Employee Participation

Relevance

Employee participation varies markedly between different parts of the world. Whereas in Japan the "joint consultation" system (Ohyama, 1984; Shimada, 1994) has not been required by law and rather initiated by company leaders, the works councils in European countries are regulated by national laws and EU regulation. In contrast to the highly institutionalized approach in the EU framework, US definitions of employee participation centre around the organizational process in which management shares influences on decision making with individual subordinates or groups of employees.

A unique form of worker participation at the corporate level is the German "co-determination" which is based on the German dual board system which divides the "Board of Directors" into a Management Board and a Supervisory Board. Co-determination law requires that half of the seats in the Supervisory Board are taken by employee representatives. The co-determination law reserves a small number of the seats to the unions, but requires democratic elections for the rest of the "employee bench", with a sub-division reserved for middle management representatives. As a result, employee representation in the Supervisory Board is not restricted to union activists. This principle also applies for works councils.

Empirical Results

In many publications, theoretical as well as empirical work, employee participation is partly understood as employee involvement in shop-floor level (and sometimes strategic) decision making and partly as "unionization". So, a study comparing employee participation in the USA and Spain (Marin García, et al. 2008) focuses on worker involvement via suggestion systems, survey feedback, job enrichment, quality circles, self-management work team and deals with union-management committees only marginally whereas others interpret employee participation as "unionization and joint union-management administration" (Cooke, 1992).

The rationale behind employee participation in form of formal cooperation between unions and management is "that productivity improvement could be attained most effectively on the basis of better mutual understanding" (Shimada, 1994, p.2) because, as a result of increased mutual trust between employees and management, the latter considers workers' needs when designing working conditions which increases workers' motivation and lowers turnover (Jirjahn, 2010, p. 9). A positive effect is, therefore, that the institutionalization of management-labor relations may reduce transaction costs. Market sceptics, however, refer to the slowness in decision making, and suspect productivity decreasing effects when "in an environment where a new technology has to be applied and where new products have to be developed and when leapfrogging to a new technology is the key task. These more radical changes, often viewed with suspicion as job-killers, conflict with the structurally conservative mindset epitomized by the institutions of codetermination." (Siebert 2004, p. 21). Empirical evidence is ambiguous. Formal representation and unionization are common in large industrial companies with high productivity levels. Addison et al. (2001), Zwick (2004), FitzRoy and Kraft (2004), Smith (2005), Renaud (2007), and Pfeifer (2011) all show a rather small but positive impact of worker participation at shop floor and board level in Germany. Better training and lower turnover which came along with worker participation may have served as catalysts. Japanese studies (for example Kato and Morishima, 2002) seem to support this result. Researchers in the United States seem to focus more on financial participation and performance-related pay – a topic not in the focus of this paper.

Non-unionized, non-formal, management-initiated employee involvement may increase productivity even more. Workers contribute with their specific knowledge of their own work, thus, being able to balance production more effectively and, as a result, eliminate bottlenecks or interruptions of the production process. They are expected to identify more with their tasks and feel more committed to work. The studies of Forde et al. (2006) and Jones et al. (2010) indicate that employee participation at the shop-floor level has a positive impact on productivity, in particular when used in combination of quality circles and teamwork. Müller (2009) points out that the productivity enhancing effect of mandatory works councils is higher when wage-negotiating union representation is organized separately. Finally, worker participation may reduce the necessity of middle management and supervision, in particular when higher cost autonomy of work groups reduces material waste and inefficiencies (Zwick, 2004).

In total, the review of empirical studies in Europe seems to support the idea of a positive relation between employee participation and productivity. However, as it was the case of the other determinants, studies are difficult to compare as the measurement of employee participation differs from study to study, mainly caused by the different forms it is codified in different countries. Moreover, the role of vocational training and employees' expectations concerning the degree of delegation and team-work related to employee participation differ from culture to culture. Thus, the results must be interpreted carefully.

8 Conclusion

In this paper, we examined selected HR-related determinants of productivity. As a first result, we found that the multitude of empirical studies has not yet led to unambiguous guidelines for companies. The major reason is that definitions and measurement of the determinants as well as productivity vary significantly. The impression after having scrutinized so many empirical research papers is that even the simple concept of productivity is not widely applied. Many studies, in particular those related to job satisfaction, do not properly distinguish between a worker's effort and job performance. Whereas the former is worker's input, the latter is the output from this effort.

Secondly, most of the studies are limited in their explanatory power as each of the determinants may be influenced by the other determinants as well as by independent factors not under control of HR policies. It is very likely, that the general economic situation and labor market conditions moderate the importance of the determinants. In times of full employment, employees may value job satisfaction more important than in times of high unemployment.

As a third result, we observed differences between studies made in the United States, Europe, and Asia. It is obvious that vocational training and re-training, employee participation, labor turnover, and job satisfaction play a different role and are perceived differently in different cultures. Further research is definitely needed for identifying the impact of culture.

In addition, none of the examined studies investigates the question to which extent the concurrence of the production factors human and physical capital determine productivity. One might assume that inadequate capital equipment alters the effect of training, turnover, job satisfaction, and participation on productivity.

These limitations also apply to our study. The restriction to the four selected variables may have limited the horizon of understanding.

This has two implications for future research. First, further analysis of already published studies should include more variables, for example non-labor determinants such as capital-endowment as well as the impact of the economic environment. Second, research on the importance of "human resources" or "human capital" for productivity may apply a more holistic approach which considers not only the impact of the determinants but also their mutual interdependence.

References

Addison, J, Schnabel, C., Wagner, J. (2001): Works Councils in Germany: Their effects on establishment performance. Oxford Economic Papers, Vol. 53, No. 4, 659-694.

Appelbaum, S. H., Adam, J., Javeri, N., Lessard, M., Lion, J.-P., Simard, M., Sorbo, S. (2005): A case study analysis of the impact of satisfaction and organizational citizenship on productivity, in: Management Research News, Vol. 28 Iss: 5, pp.1 – 26.

Ariga, K., Kurosawa, M., Ohtake, F., Sasaki, M., Yamane, S. (2013): Organization Adjustments, Job training and Productivity: Evidence from Japanese Automobile Makers. Journal of the Japanese and International Economies, Vol. 27, 1-34.

Bartel, A. (2000): Measuring the Employer's Return on Investments in Training: Evidence from the Literature. Industrial Relations, Vol. 39, No. 3, 502-524.

Böckerman, P., Ilmakunnas, P. (2010): The job satisfaction-productivity nexus: A study using matched survey and register data. HECER Discussion Paper No. 297.

Bossaert, D. (2005): The flexibilisation of the employment status of civil servants: From life tenure to more flexible employment relations? European Institute of Public Administration. http://www.eupan.eu/files/repository/03_The_flexibilisation_of_the_employment_status_of_civil_servants.pdf; retrieved Feb 22, 2016.

Chen, T.Y., Chang P.L., Yeh, C.W. (2004): An investigation of career development programs, job satisfaction, professional development and productivity: the case of Taiwan, in: Human Resource Development International, Vol. 4, No.4, pp.441-4633.

Christen, M., Iyer, G., Soberman, D. (2006): Job satisfaction, job performance, and effort: A reexamination using agency theory, in: Journal of Marketing, Vil. 70, No. 1, pp. 137-150.

Colombo, E., Stanca, L. (2014): The impact of training on productivity: evidence from a panel of Italian firms. International Journal of Manpower, Vol. 35, No. 8, 1140 – 1158.

Conti, G. (2005): Training, productivity and wages in Italy. Labour Economics. Vol. 12, No. 4, 557-576.

Cooke, W. N. (1992): Product Quality Improvement through Employee Participation: The Effects of Unionization and Joint Union-Management Administration, in: Industrial & Labor Relations Review, Vol- 46, pp. 119-134.

Cooper, D. (2001): Innovation and Reciprocal Externalities: Information Transmission via Job Mobility. Journal of Economic Behavior and Organizations, Vol. 45, No. 4, 403-425.

EUROFOUND (2007) – European Foundation for the Improvement of Living and Working Conditions, Dublin, https://www.eurofound.europa.eu//sites/default/files/ef_files/ewco/reports/TN0608TR01/TN0608TR01.pdf, retrieved February 24th, 2016.

FitzRoy, F., Kraft, K. (2004): Co-determination, Efficiency, and Productivity. IZA Discussion Paper, No. 1442.

Forde, C., Slater, G., Spencer, D.A. (2006): It's the Taking Part that Counts? Participation, Performance and External Labour Market Conditions. Relations Industrielles/Industrial Relations, Vol. 61, No. 2, 296-320.

Halkos, G., Bousinakis, D. (2010): The Effect of Stress and Satisfaction on Productivity, in: International Journal of Productivity and Performance Management, Vol. 59, pp. 415-431.

Hancock, J., David G. Allen, D.G., Bosco, F.A., McDaniel, K.R., Pierce, C.A. (2013): Meta-Analytic Review of Employee Turnover as a Predictor of Firm Performance. Journal of Management, Vol. 39, 573-609.

Hansen and Wernerfelt (1989): Determinants of Firm Performance: The Relative Importance of Economic and Organizational Factors. Strategic Management Journal, Vol. 10, No. 5, pp. 399-411.

Hara, H. (2014): The impact of firm-provided training on productivity, wages, and transition to regular employment for workers in flexible arrangements. Journal of the Japanese and International Economies, Volume 34, 336–359

Holtom, B.C., Mitchell, T.R., Lee, T.W., Eberly, M.B. (2008): Turnover and Retention Research: A Glance at the Past, a Closer View of the Present, and a Venture into the Future. The Academy of Management Annals, Vol. 2, No. 1, 231-274.

Jirjahn, U. (2010): Ökonomische Wirkungen der Mitbestimmung in Deutschland: Ein Update. Arbeitspapier 186. Wirtschaft und Finanzen. Hans-Böckler-Stiftung.

Jones, D.C., Kalmi, P., Kauhanen, A. (2010): How Does Employee Involvement Stack Up? The Effects of Human Resource Management Policies on Performance in a Retail Firm. Industrial Relations: A Journal of Economy and Society, Vol. 49, No. 1, 1-21.

Jorgenson, D.W. (1966): The Embodiment Hypothesis. Journal of Political Economy, Vol. 74, No. 1, 1-17.

Judge, T., A., Thoresen, C. J., Bono, J. C., Patton, G. K. (2001): The Job Satisfaction-Job Performance Relationship: A Qualitative and Quantitative Review, in: Psychological Bulletin, Vol. 127. No. 3, pp. 376-407

Kato, T., Morishima, M. (2002): The Productivity Effects of Participatory Employment Practices: Evidence from New Japanese Panel Data. Industrial Relations: A Journal of Economy and Society, Vol. 41, No. 4, 487–520.

Kim, Y., Ployhart, R.E. (2014): The effects of staffing and training on firm productivity and profit growth before, during, and after the Great Recession. Journal of Applied Psychology, Vol. 99, No. 3, 361-389.

Maliranta, M., Asplund, R. (2007): Training and Hiring Strategies to Improve Firm Performance. ETLA Discussion Papers No. 1105.

Marin-García, J. A., Bonavia, T., Miralles, C. (2008): The use of employee participation in the USA and Spanish companies, in: International Journal of Management Science and Engineering Management, Vol. 3, pp. 71-80.

Müller, K.; Peters, B. (2010): Churning of R&D Personnel and Innovation. ZEW Discussion Paper No. 10-032.

Müller, S. (2009): Mandatory Works Councils in Germany: Their Effects on Productivity and Profits. Doctoral Dissertation.

Ohyama, N. (1984): Workers' Participation in Management as an Ambivalent Process: A Japanese Case. Hokkaido University Collection of Scholarly and Academic Papers 22_P1-17.

Parrotta, P., Pozzoli, D. (2012): The effect of learning by hiring on productivity. The RAND Journal of Economics, Vol. 43, No 1, 167–185.

Ramlall, S. (2003): Managing Employee Retention as a Strategy for Increasing Organizational Competitiveness, in: Applied H.R.M. Research, Vol. 8, 63-72.

Renaud, S. (2007): Dynamic Efficiency of Supervisory Board Codetermination in Germany. LABOUR, Vol. 21, No 4-5, 689–712.

Romer, P.M. (1989): Human Capital and Growth: Theory and Evidence. NBER Working Paper No. 3173.

Rose, M. (2001): Disparate measures in the workplace. Quantifying overall job satisfaction, BHPS Research Conference, Colchester, 2001.

Sala, J., Silva, J. (2013): Labor productivity and vocational training: evidence from Europe. Journal of Productivity Analysis, Vol. 40, No. 1, 31-41.

Scarpetta, S. (2014): Employment Protection. IZA World of Labor. http://wol.iza.org/articles/employment-protection/long

Sepúlveda, F. (2010): Training and productivity: evidence for US manufacturing industries. Oxford Economic Papers, Vol. 62, No. 3, 504-528.

Shaw, J.D., Gupta, N., Delery, J.E. (2005): Alternative Conceptualizations of the Relations between Voluntary Turnover and Organizational Performance. Academy of Management Journal, Vol. 48, Vol. 1, 50-68.

Shaw, J.D., Duffy, M., Johnson, J., Lockhart, D. (2005a): Turnover, Social Capital Losses, and Performance. Academy of Management Journal, Vol. 48, No. 4, 594-606.

Shimada, H. (1994): Worker Participation in Management Decision Making. Cornell University ILR School, Digital   Commons@ILR http://digitalcommons.ilr.cornell.edu/cgi/viewcontent.cgi?article=1432&context=key_workplace,   retrieved February 21, 2016

Siebert, H. (2004): Economic and Political Governance in Germany's Social Market Economy Kiel Institute for World Economics: Working Paper No. 1207.

Siebert, S., Zubanov, N. (2009): Searching for The Optimal Level of Employee Turnover: A Study of a Large U.K. Retail Organization. Academy of Management Journal, Vol. 52, 294-313.

Smith, S. (2006): Employee Participation Rights in Corporate Governance: An Economic Rationale, a Test of a Leading Theory, and Some Initial Policy Proposals, in: Kalmi, P., Klinedinst, M. (ed.) Participation in the Age of Globalization and Information (Advances in the Economic Analysis of Participatory & Labor-Managed Firms, Volume 9), 105 – 146.

Solow, R.M. (1962): Technical Progress, Capital Formation, and Economic Growth. The American Economic Review, Vol. 52, No. 2, 76-86.

Sousa-Poza, A., & Sousa-Poza, A. A. (2000). Well-being at work: a cross-national analysis of the levels and determinants of job satisfaction. The Journal of Socio-economics, 29(6), 517-538.

Spector, P. E. (1985): Measurement of Human Service Staff Satisfaction: Development of the Job Satisfaction Survey, in: American Journal of Community Psychology, Vol. 13, 693-713.

Spector, P. E. (1997): Job satisfaction: Application, assessment, causes, and consequences, Sage.

Spector, P. E. (2016): Job Satisfaction Survey, http://shell.cas.usf.edu/~pspector/scales/jsspag.html, retrieved February 24th, 2016.

Tharenou, P., Saks, A.M., Moore, C. (2007): A review and critique of research on training and organizational-level outcomes. Human Resource Management Review, Vol. 17, No. 3, 251–273.

Topel, R. (1999): Labor Markets and Economic Growth, in: Ashenfelter, O., Card, D., Handbook of Labor Economics. Elsevier.

Westlund, A., Loethgren, M. (2001): The Interactions between Quality, Productivity and Economic Performance: the Case of Swedish Pharmacies, in: Total Quality Management, Vol. 12, no.3, pp. 385-396.

Wu, W.Y., Tsai, C.C., Fu, C.S. (2013): The relationship among internal marketing, job satisfaction, relationship marketing, customer orientation, and organizational performance: An empirical study of TFT-LCD companies in Taiwan, in: Human Factors and Ergonomics in Manufacturing and Services Industries, Vol. 23, No. 5, pp. 436-449.

Yazinski, S. K. (2009): Strategies for Retaining Employees and Minimizing Turnover, in: HR.BLR.com. Compliance Tools for HR Managers: https://hr.blr.com/whitepapers/Staffing-Training/Employee-Turnover/Strategies-for-Retaining-Employees-and-Minimizing

Zwick, T. (2004): Employee Participation and Productivity, in: Labour Economics, Vol. 11, No. 6, 715-740.

Zwick, T. (2005): Continuing Vocational Training Forms and Establishment Productivity in Germany. German Economic Review, Vol. 6, No. 2, 155–184.

7 LEAN HR MANAGEMENT – IMPLEMENTATION INTO PRACTICE

Carolin Grode

TABLE OF CONTENTS

Abstract

This chapter provides a practical insight into the topic of Lean HR Management. First, the necessity of aligning HR services more effectively to customer's needs is outlined. Then the origin and fundamentals of the Lean Management philosophy are explained and critical voices of applying the production-based approach to the personnel division are commented. Finally, framework conditions of successfully transferring lean principles to Human Resources departments are described which are based on the professional experience of the author as HR Project Manager and Lean HR Specialist.

Mail contact: carolin.heide@gmail.com

1   Introduction

Nowadays personnel departments face the challenge to closely align the HR services to their customer's needs but also make a significant value contribution to the business by providing individual support within a shorter period of time and with less HR staff (Schönenberg, 2010, p. 14). Lean HR Management is one option to handle the balancing act between optimizing customers' satisfaction and reducing HR efforts. However, there is no precise definition of Lean HR Management procedures that can easily be applied by every organization. Currently very rare significant best practice examples can be found on Lean HR Management. Although there is a lot of professional literature of Lean Production, the framework conditions of shop floors vary from those of the administrative areas. Therefore, a one-on-one implementation of lean production techniques in HR is not reasonable.

The challenge exists in transferring only greater success-promising lean methods from the production area to the personnel division. The skepticism amongst HR professionals towards Lean HR Management still exists. Therefore, it's crucial to consider both, a balanced cost-benefit-ratio of applying Lean Management and to apply well selected optimization methods that have been accepted by the HR workforce. Lean HR Management can be implemented effectively and sustainably also in HR departments only if the benefits of the Japanese philosophy of continuous improvement can be made visible for personnel departments as well. Fortunately, in modern HR organization the topic "Lean HR Management", "Operational Excellence" or "HR Optimization" gains more recognition as Lean Management methods and Lean Thinking techniques are applied. However, one question remains: "Which framework conditions need to be considered when applying Lean Management in the HR department?" To answer this question, it's vital to understand the extent to which Lean Management principles should be adapted to the HR department and the necessity of HR optimization.

2   Necessity and options for optimizing Human Resources Management

The most obvious reason for constantly improving business activities dates back to the concept of being a modern, flexible and profitable organization in order to be well prepared in succeeding in market conditions and ensuring a longtime company existence. Not only production units and departments with intensive external customer contact like the units of Sales and Purchasing are requested to increase the value contribution to the business, but also purely cost-driven functions such as the Personnel Division have to increase productivity. As a service unit the focus for HR must lie primarily on customers' interests, in addition to legal and institutional regulations. The challenge is to fulfill and even exceed the client's expectations considering aspects of time, quality and service costs in a well-balanced manner, see figure 1. Hence, HR must closely align processes to customer's needs and provide services faster by utilizing HR information systems and thereby having less staff.

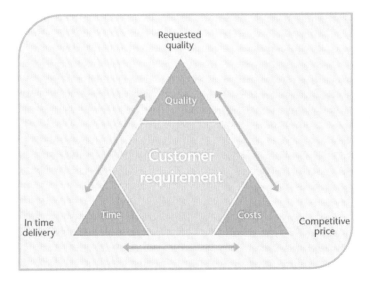

Figure 1: Triangle of Customer Requirements

Modern customer service also implies that the HR representatives become more responsible for the outcome of the service and have closer and more proactive contact to their clients. Eventually the satisfaction of the customer and the ability of the HR partner to increase service quality will rise. Of course, there are other undertakings that have been well-established during the recent years, often mentioned by the keyword of "Operational Excellence". Reducing the workforce to comply with certain market benchmarks and to arrive at a good HR service quota[9] represents common practices. In recent years many enterprises replaced local IT systems with a singular harmonized HR IT platform or with HR Shared Services to steer the main HR procedures centrally and increase data quality. Efforts for standardizing and professionalizing work processes by consolidating similar HR activities and reducing unnecessary tasks have also been applied more often and already point towards Lean Management thinking.

The crucial aspect and fundamental difference between optimization initiatives and implementing Lean HR Management is speed. Harmonized HR IT systems and a shared services portfolio quickly result in optimized processes, including system landscape and a less cost-intensive number of staff. However, it also causes a tremendous turbulence in the organization and thereby also poses a significant risk of failure and overall cost increase. That's why, implementation must consist of small steps on the latter of improvement to accomplish Operational Excellence sustainably in the long run. The Lean Management philosophy supports the continuous optimization of HR business activities by aligning not just major HR processes and systems but by also fostering the individual improvement of every HR employee step-by-step.

Lean Management is more than a technique but rather an approach to think self-reflectively and from the perspective of the customer instead of keeping existing HR services as they are just because they always worked in the past. Lean Management focuses on optimizing only activities that are proven necessary for business sustainability.

---

[9] HR service quota = Percentage of employees served by one HR representative

110

3   Theory of Lean Management

The approach „Lean Management" defines a method for realizing continuous improvement in every department, organizational unit and process within a company by identifying sources for waste and ensuring their elimination. Lean Management is also seen to be a philosophy that has lived by the employees of an organization on a daily basis in order to realize significant optimizations on a long-term basis (Pfeiffer/ Werner/Weiss 1994, pp. 3). Lean Management has its origin in the Toyota Production System (TPS) which was developed by the Japanese engineers Eiji Toyoda and Taiichi Ohno (2009, pp. 14) in the 60/70s They proposed to re-organize the manufacturing areas at the Toyota Motor Corporation to a so called "Lean Production" in order to compete with the strong US car producer market. The manufacturing method of Toyota incorporated elements of the quality approach called Total Quality Management (Appel & Felisiak, 2011, p. 139) and the theory of structural process organizations (Kosiol, 1976, pp. 32). Under consideration of optimizing all manufacturing procedures, TPS was designed to ensure the long-term existence of Toyota during the post-war period when the mass production of the western car producing industry was almost almighty (Stoeff & Schmeisser, 2014, pp. 9). KAIZEN is the foundation of Toyoda's philosophy of sustainable improvement and symbolizes the constant striving for an improved status. Since *KAI* stands for Change and *ZEN* for Better, KAIZEN can be summarized as "Change for the better". Hence, every HR service, process, system and employee can change to become better when living according to the KAIZEN mentality through a fundamental grasp of Lean Management.

Lean Management focuses on optimizing activities that result in a benefit for the customer and eliminating activities that are not demanded by the clients. Activities that are not supportive or requested are called "Types of Waste" and have to be identified in order to reduce them as much as possible (Wagner & Lindner, 2013, p. 3). Waste is the most obvious course for ineffective and unused potentials, see examples in table 1.

Table 1: Types of Waste with examples and possible consequences

Type of Waste	Examples	Possible consequence
Overproduction / Over administration	High complexity of data, Widely ramified structure of folders	Lose overview
High stocks	Oversized archive of documents	Cause costs
Errors	Wrong procedures applied, Insufficient data collected	Need extra work
Double work	Multiple people work at the same customer request where only one person is needed	Trigger demotivation
Interfaces	Uncertainty about needed information, Lack of communication	Initiate mis-understandings
Long ways	Long walking distances between frequently interacting departments	Waste time
Waiting times	Poor system performance, slow mode of operation by previously processing employee	Decrease speed
Non-utilized talent	Unused richness of ideas due to too much routine work, Standard procedures	Suppress employee creativity

All Lean approaches underlie the same principle of optimization which is the Continuous Improvement Process (CIP). The focus lies on the customer's requirements which always have to be satisfied by constantly adapting the product, service or process accordingly (Kostka & Kostka, 2008,p. 12). With the help of the cyclic procedure "Plan, Do, Check, Act" a structured CIP is ensured and provides a manageable tool for almost every employee in every department to improve work routines self-responsibly. "Plan" defines the problem and plans necessary actions, "Do" focuses on implementing the actions, "Check" deals with verifying in how far the actions influenced the goal attainment and "Act" examines successful actions that can be defined as standards. Besides also considering further actions that need to be implemented it also serves as a starting signal for the next planning stage.

4   Sceptics towards Lean Management in HR practice

With regard to human nature, it's quite normal that HR specialists react with skepticism when they see themselves confronted with a production methodology like Lean Management. Many of them argue that it seems as if they would invest valuable energy into an apparently off-topic by devoting themselves to Lean methodologies. Many practitioners think that Lean is simply not applicable in the administrative units especially in the HR department. This prejudgment is based on the fact that there is neither a significant definition of Lean HR Management nor precise descriptions of applying Lean actions in the HR organization as there is for production units. Also trained employees conclude that Lean Management might be applicable to some enterprises but not to their own organization (Liker & Meier, 2013, pp. 63).

Many conclude that Lean Management does not work in a HR department as it is a production-oriented approach is persistent as Lean Management derives from the Toyoda Production System and is focused on the optimization of manufacturing procedures in the automotive industry. Moreover, Lean initiatives are often misunderstood as a restructuring measure, because the HR function is operating as a cost center and can therefore most effectively influence the business turnover by staff cutbacks and reduction of employee compensation (Lay, 2013, p. 43). This is the primary reason for the great reluctance when Lean Management is proposed for HR optimization.

Another misconception exists in the false belief that Lean Management always demands linear processes, because every manufacturing process of a product follows a precise production stream, none of which can be left out. Therefore, in the manufacturing unit processes mainly run linear and follow strict chronological sequences while the process in the HR departments have to be flexible in order to satisfy the customers' needs.

Additionally, Lean Management is based on measuring results with hard facts which seems impossible for the HR function. However, in the Personnel division the precise data collection of Lean Management KPIs is not applicable or is regarded to be too difficult. Processes in administration cannot always be measured as detailed as in the production environment that breaks down the overall lead time into process time, transfer time, feedback time, system time and others. It's argued that the assessment of this data will cause more time than waste can be reduced, also because HR processes run through less standardization than manufacturing procedures.

In order to eliminate prejudices, it must be omitted that the framework conditions of shop floors vary from those of the administrative areas. In the same breath it has to be clearly stated that Lean Management principles also apply to HR although a one-on-one implementation is not necessarily reasonable. The key to success lies in an appropriate adaptation of the Lean Management philosophy to the departmental circumstances. The basic principles of Lean Management hold true for HR departments as well as especially the CIP-approach (Plan, Do, Check, Act), the elimination of waste types and the benefits of the Flow Principle which stands for a continuous flow with lowest possible amount of information through the whole value stream. The core elements of these concepts are applicable to each unit of an enterprise because all organizational units are aligned in the same core target that is to focus on clients' needs and only provide the necessary to reach full customer satisfaction. In addition, processes don't necessarily demand linear processes, but they request a certain degree of repetitiveness. In order to optimize processes they don't need to follow a strict linear chronological order as long as they are of repetitive character and follow a standard approach. A certain level of standardization is ensured automatically. As soon as a HR process repeats several times during a fiscal year, month, week or day and can therefore be analyzed according to the criteria of Lean

Management. Finally, it's highly recommendable to underpin the results of all optimization efforts by well-established methods of quality assurance in order to make improvements measurable and visible to the employees involved (Jekiel, 2011, p. 161). Lean Management KPIs that also work for HR interventions are for instance lead time, customer satisfaction and disturbance-free operation.

However, until Lean Management is as well established in the administration departments like it has been for decades in the production units, a lot of irritation and insecurity will exist among HR representatives that should be taken seriously. Therefore, professional Lean Specialists will have to consider Change Management aspects to face sceptics with broad perspective, patience and a profound line of argumentation.

5   Framework conditions for applying Lean HR Management

Lean Management principles can be applied successfully to the HR function. However, the manner of application depends on the organizational and cultural situation of the company. Therefore, the challenge of implementing Lean Management sustainably exists in defining appropriate framework conditions and then choosing the most appropriate way of action. Effective Lean techniques will differ from organization to organization, but the preconditions remain the same.

The following recommendations for supportive framework conditions represent the personal lessons learned by the author. As a HR Project Manager and Lean HR Specialist she was involved into and responsible for various international HR projects during her employment as at a globally represented technology group in the areas of specialty glass in the B2B business, including pharmaceutical, electronical, optical, automotive and aviation industries.

Cleary structured process landscape is needed to work process-oriented. To start with, it needs a clearly defined process landscape that considers all main HR processes, hierarchical levels as well as information about the incorporation into the entire HR organizational structure. This map supports the process-oriented approach instead of the department-oriented approach. By understanding the process instead of how the members of the department work, it takes the focus away from the employee's performance and yields at the process layout. Advantages of utilizing a process-oriented approach include higher motivation of the HR staff to support the project and more transparency in procedures and responsibilities. The latter one is ensured by defining a clearly structured process map with process owners. An even more relevant advantage of the process map is the fact that it supports the analysis of end-to-end processes which is more goal-oriented since clients demand a certain service regardless of which unit is working on it. Therefore, the whole process has to be understood and optimized in the long run for which a significant process landscape is an indispensable prerequisite for each process optimization.

Processes with high repetition rate best highlight lean effects. The categorization of each HR process according to its frequency that it repeats within a calendar year is crucial to distinguish between the process manners. In order to define highly repetitive processes, an appropriate scale needs to be define e.g. process loops >50 times/year or >twice/week. It's of decisive importance to start with focusing on HR processes with a high repetition frequency, because the effects of improvement actions taken become visible quicker than with seldom repeating processes. Especially during the phase of Lean Management implementation, it's beneficial to focus on HR processes with high repetition to disclose and eliminate types of waste. Outcomes of Lean interventions are displayed almost immediately and will create lighthouse effects through prompt adjustment according to the CIP-principle.

The Leadership team takes over the role as sponsor of Lean HR Management. The HR leadership team has to act as a role model in living the principles of Lean Management and exhibiting the way of behavior according to lean philosophy. This is because the majority of employees will more quickly be convinced by supervisors that apply the methodology themselves that they proclaim. Only through a repeated and long-dated usage, the KAIZEN mentality can be deeply understood and deployed sustainably by the HR workforce and thereby generate real impact to the optimization of the HR service.

Relevant KPIs ensure certainty about progress by everyone involved. Prior to applying the first Lean Management technique, data of key performance indicators (KPI) that were defined together with the Lean Management sponsors have to be collected to reflect the status quo. KPIs may be determined with regard to time, inputs/resources, costs, errors, satisfaction and any other individual subject to improvement. After lean actions have been implemented, the validation of key measures ensure transparency for everyone involved concerning the current situation and the next step to an optimized stage. Hence, clearly defined metrics help to prevent people from working in different directions, at worst in opposite ones and disclose the grounds of project's performance measurement from the beginning forward.

Acceptance of Lean techniques is more profitable than effectiveness of the method. Before starting to deploy success promising Lean techniques it's advisable to find out about the employee's affirmation of Lean Management. It's important to be familiar with the level of sceptics and consent, because the methods of Lean have to be accepted by the HR workforce before any potential of optimization can be exploited. It might be the case that certain techniques are more accepted by the workforce than others due to previous knowledge, cultural conditions or personal attitude. The acceptance of a lean intervention is as least as important as a high level of effectiveness and even to be prioritized in case of disaccord. This is because it's more important to get Lean Management started with the employees' participation than to realize more convincing optimization results without the staffs buy-in. In first instance Lean Management has to work on the operational level and must be of use for the employees involved in the process. In case of employee uncertainty or personal restraints the active support by Lean experts in the selection and application of suitable Lean actions is a wise choice. However, it's more advantageous to get people actively involved and let them implement lean practices themselves, because the positive experience made will be a motivator to continue with Lean in the long run.

Discipline in structuring Lean intervention helps to handle potential complexity. It goes without saying that complex projects are structured with great detail, but also small Lean interventions need to follow a planned cause of action. Over administration

117

and extensive documentation is not worthwhile and will cause additional waste. However, it's most helpful to invest some time in thinking through a Lean project to the end and taking reasonable care in making notes although the Lean action might be less complex. Well-structured manuals will offer the flexibility to often and quickly adapt the way of proceeding without losing track on what had been done already and for which reasons. What is more, small designed lean interventions very often become large scale projects that require much less resources if a thorough documentation already exists. That's why it's smart to apply a structured planning and documentation approach for every Lean intervention as a matter of principle.

The most important rule is to keep continuing with Lean Management activities. Depending on the organizational surrounding, the implementation of Lean Management will be more or less challenging. Undoubtedly, active support by the management, the availability of resources and an open-minded and self-critical workforce will have a beneficial effect on the progress and outcome of the first Lean activity. However, as also outlined in the previous chapters many HR professionals are reluctant to Lean Management. Hence, the process of deploying a structured approach of becoming operationally excellent can be energy-snapping before first Lean results help questioning conventional patterns of thinking. However, it's crucial to understand that it's not enough to install a lighthouse project and enable the employees to apply Lean technique. The real task exists in carrying on with Lean Management continuously (see figure 2), since Lean Management has to become a part of the organizational culture to sustainably see the benefits of fully optimized processes, systems and team work.

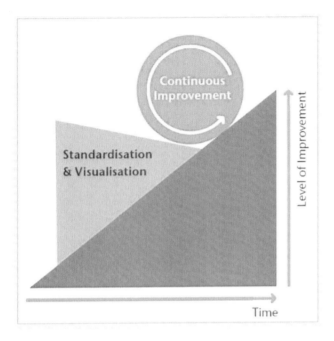

Figure 2: Standardization as basis for further improvement

While continuously adapting to customer needs and improving existing structures, it's important to set standards which means to freeze the status quo of proven procedures. These standards will function as basis for further improvement since it's a fact that as long as customers change their minds and markets develop, companies need to keep with the evolving requirements and expectations. Thus, modern HR departments have to ensure a high level of knowledge, secure further development of processes and systems and will need to avoid the recurrence of faults in order to stay competitive in the long run.

References

Appel, W. & Felisiak, W. (2011). HR-Servicemanagement: Produktion von Personalservices. Oldenbourg Verlag.

Jekiel, C. M. (2011). Lean Human Resources: Redesigning HR Processes for a Culture of Continuous Improvement. Productivity Press.

Kosiol, E. (1976). Organisation der Unternehmung, Wiesbaden: Betriebswirtschaftlicher Verlag Gabler.

Kostka, C. & Kostka, S. (2008). Der kontinuierliche Verbesserungsprozess. München.

Lay, D. (2013). Lean HR: Introducing process excellence to your practice.

Liker, J. K. & Meier, D. P. (2013). Der Toyota Weg: Praxisbuch für jedes Unternehmen. München: Finanzbuch Verlag.

Ōhno, T. (2009). Das Toyota-Produktionssystem. Frankfurt, M./New York, NY: Campus-Verlag.

Prof. Dr. Pfeiffer, W. & Weiss, E. (1994). Lean-Management: Grundlagen der Führung und Organisation lernender Unternehmen. Berlin: Erich Schmidt.

Schönenberg, U. (2010). Prozessexzellenz im HR-Management: Professionelle Prozesse mit dem HR-Management Maturity Model. Berlin/New York: Springer.

Stoeff, D. & Schmeisser, W. (2014). Lean Management: Management konkret. Konstanz. UVK Verlagsgesellschaft mbH.

Wagner, K. W. & Lindner, A. M. (2013). WPM-Wertstromorientiertes Prozessmanagement: Effizienz steigern, Verschwendung reduzieren, Abläufe optimieren. München. Carl Hanser Verlag.